Language

Themes 62

Performance 68

Skills and Practice 84

Glossary 94

Introduction

What are Oxford Literature Companions?

Oxford Literature Companions is a series designed to provide you with comprehensive support for popular set texts. You can use the Companion alongside your play, using relevant sections during your studies or using the book as a whole for revision.

This Companion includes detailed guidance and practical activities on:

- **Plot and Structure**
- **Context**
- **Characters**
- **Language**
- **Themes**
- **Performance**
- **Skills and Practice**

How does this book help with exam preparation?

As well as providing guidance on key areas of the play, throughout this book you will also find 'Upgrade' features. These are tips to help you prepare for your assessment.

In addition, the **Skills and Practice** chapter provides detailed guidance on areas such as approaching your revision, understanding essay and extract-based questions, planning written answers and using quotations.

In the **Skills and Practice** chapter there is also a bank of **Sample questions** and **Sample answers**. The **Sample answers** are marked and include annotations and a summative comment.

How does this book help with terminology?

Throughout the book, key terms are **highlighted** in the text and explained on the same page. There is also a detailed **Glossary** at the end of the book that explains, in the context of the novel, all the relevant terms highlighted in this book.

How does this book work?

Each book in the Oxford Literature Companions series follows the same approach and includes the following features:

- **Key quotations** from the novel
- **Key terms** explained on the page and linked to a complete glossary at the end of the book
- **Activity boxes** to help improve your understanding of the text
- **Upgrade** tips to help prepare you for your assessment

To help illustrate the features in this book, here are two annotated pages taken from this Oxford Literature Companion:

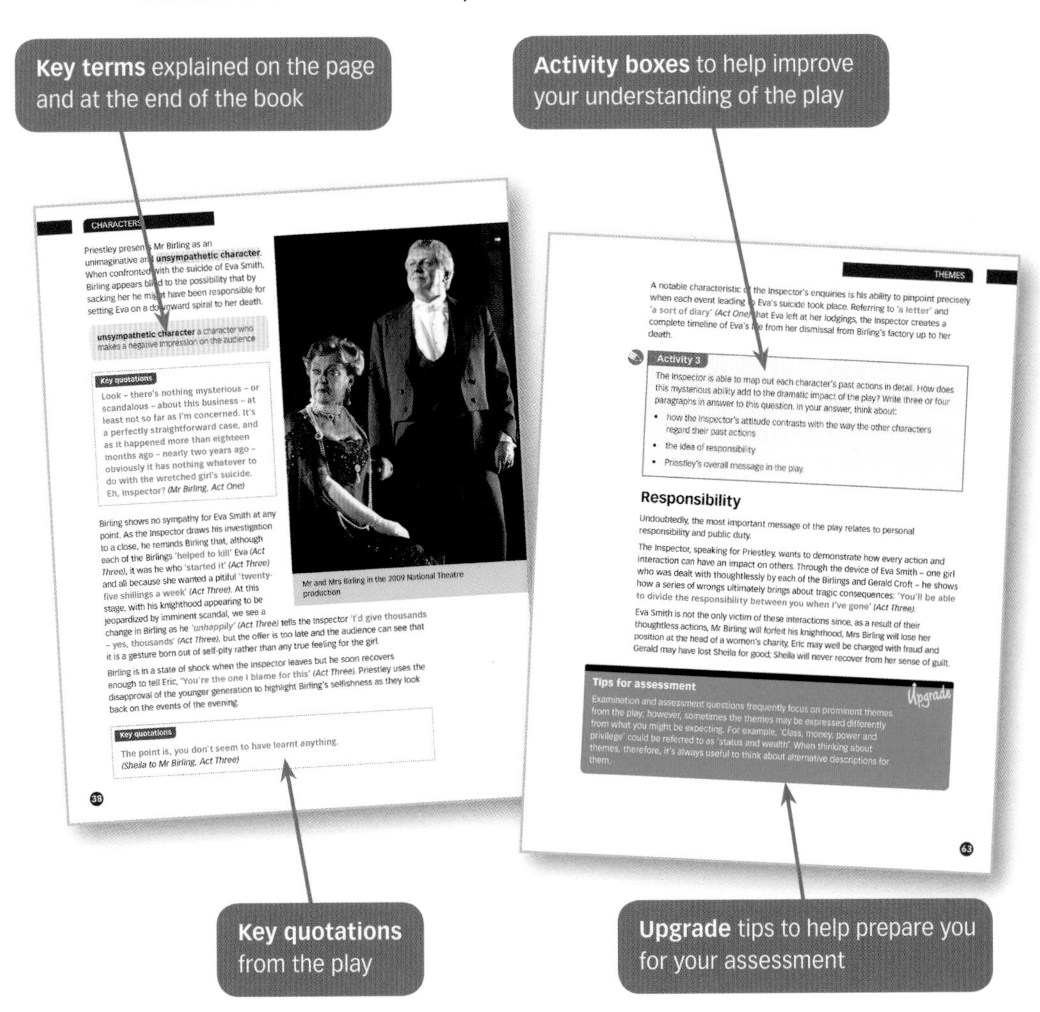

CHARACTERS

Priestley presents Mr Birling as an unimaginative and **unsympathetic character**. When confronted with the suicide of Eva Smith, Birling appears blind to the possibility that by sacking her he might have been responsible for setting Eva on a downward spiral to her death.

unsympathetic character a character who makes a negative impression on the audience

Key quotations

Look – there's nothing mysterious – or scandalous – about this business – at least not so far as I'm concerned. It's a perfectly straightforward case, and as it happened more than eighteen months ago – nearly two years ago – obviously it has nothing whatever to do with the wretched girl's suicide. Eh, Inspector? *(Mr Birling, Act One)*

Mr and Mrs Birling in the 2009 National Theatre production

Birling shows no sympathy for Eva Smith at any point. As the Inspector draws his investigation to a close, he reminds Birling that, although each of the Birlings 'helped to kill' Eva *(Act Three)*, it was he who 'started it' *(Act Three)* and all because she wanted a pitiful 'twenty-five shillings a week' *(Act Three)*. At this stage, with his knighthood appearing to be jeopardized by imminent scandal, we see a change in Birling as he *'unhappily' (Act Three)* tells the Inspector 'I'd give thousands – yes, thousands' *(Act Three)*, but the offer is too late and the audience can see that it is a gesture born out of self-pity rather than any true feeling for the girl.

Birling is in a state of shock when the Inspector leaves but he soon recovers enough to tell Eric, 'You're the one I blame for this' *(Act Three)*. Priestley uses the disapproval of the younger generation to highlight Birling's selfishness as they look back on the events of the evening.

Key quotations

The point is, you don't seem to have learnt anything. *(Sheila to Mr Birling, Act Three)*

38

THEMES

A notable characteristic of the Inspector's enquiries is his ability to pinpoint precisely when each event leading to Eva's suicide took place. Referring to 'a letter' and 'a sort of diary' *(Act One)* that Eva left at her lodgings, the Inspector creates a complete timeline of Eva's life from her dismissal from Birling's factory up to her death.

Activity 3

The Inspector is able to map out each character's past actions in detail. How does this mysterious ability add to the dramatic impact of the play? Write three or four paragraphs in answer to this question. In your answer, think about:

- how the Inspector's attitude contrasts with the way the other characters regard their past actions
- the idea of responsibility
- Priestley's overall message in the play.

Responsibility

Undoubtedly, the most important message of the play relates to personal responsibility and public duty.

The Inspector, speaking for Priestley, wants to demonstrate how every action and interaction can have an impact on others. Through the device of Eva Smith – one girl who was dealt with thoughtlessly by each of the Birlings and Gerald Croft – he shows how a series of wrongs ultimately brings about tragic consequences: 'You'll be able to divide the responsibility between you when I've gone' *(Act Three)*.

Eva Smith is not the only victim of these interactions since, as a result of their thoughtless actions, Mr Birling will forfeit his knighthood, Mrs Birling will lose her position at the head of a women's charity, Eric may well be charged with fraud and Gerald may have lost Sheila for good; Sheila will never recover from her sense of guilt.

Tips for assessment

Upgrade

Examination and assessment questions frequently focus on prominent themes from the play; however, sometimes the themes may be expressed differently from what you might be expecting. For example, 'Class, money, power and privilege' could be referred to as 'status and wealth'. When thinking about themes, therefore, it's always useful to think about alternative descriptions for them.

63

Plot

The play is divided into three **Acts**. For the purposes of this book, however, these have been divided into individual episodes, reflecting the progress of the Inspector's 'investigation' of the Birling family – one member at a time.

Act One

Episode 1 – The Engagement party

This section begins with the stage directions at the beginning of Act One: ***'The dining-room of a fairly large suburban house…'*** *(Act One)*.

As the play opens, a family dinner celebrating the engagement of two characters, Sheila and Gerald, is drawing to a close. We meet Sheila's father Mr Arthur Birling, a wealthy factory owner, her mother Sybil and her brother Eric. We also meet Gerald, the son of Birling's business rival, Sir George Croft.

Gerald presents Sheila with a beautiful engagement ring and Mr Birling proposes a toast to the couple. Speaking about the future, based on his experience as a **'hard-headed, practical man of business'** *(Act One)*, Mr Birling predicts a time of peace and prosperity for **capitalists** like himself.

After the speeches, Mrs Birling, Sheila and Eric withdraw to another room, leaving Mr Birling and Gerald to enjoy another glass of port.

- Gerald gives Sheila an engagement ring – a symbol of love and trust – both important ideas in the play; later, Sheila returns the ring.
- Birling's predictions about the future are important because the audience knows that they will be proved wrong. The audience can appreciate the **dramatic irony** of Birling's 'certainty' about the coming years.
- Birling ridicules the ideas of writers with **socialist** sympathies such as George Bernard Shaw and H.G. Wells. Significantly, these are writers whom Priestley admired very much.

Act the name given to the major divisions of a play

capitalist society a society where individuals can own and run businesses to make profit; to be successful, business owners must compete to keep costs low (e.g. paying the lowest possible wages) while selling their products for the highest possible price

dramatic irony where the audience have greater knowledge than the characters on stage, enabling them to judge and react to events based on their superior understanding

socialist society a society that is based on the cooperative ownership and running of businesses, where profits are shared among all the people involved

Key facts about early 20th-century writers

George Bernard Shaw (1856–1950) was an Irish playwright and a prominent member of the Fabian Society, which supported equal rights for men and women and fair treatment of the working class. His plays regularly deal with such social issues.

H.G. Wells (1866–1946) was an English author who is best known for his science-fiction novels but he also wrote about history, politics and war. He was a committed socialist; his views on the inevitability of a world state, run on socialist lines, are what Birling is so scathing about.

Activity 1

1. Re-read Birling's predictions for the future from the opening of the play. Create a table to show what each prediction reveals about Mr Birling and his views about what is important in life.
2. Why do you think Priestley focuses on 'the future' so early in the play?

Episode 2 – Birling and Gerald talk alone

This section begins with the exit of Mrs Birling, Sheila and Eric, leaving Mr Birling alone with Gerald.

Mr Birling privately tries to impress Gerald with news of his forthcoming knighthood. He hopes this will please Gerald's mother Lady Croft, who, he feels, disapproves of Gerald's engagement to Sheila.

Mr Birling and Gerald in the 2009 National Theatre production

Eric returns and helps himself to another drink. Mr Birling offers the young men some advice about life. He is discussing a person's responsibility to **'look after himself and his own'** *(Act One)* when a doorbell interrupts him and the arrival of the Inspector is announced.

- Birling and Gerald enjoy another glass of port and a smoke, showing they are used to indulging themselves. The differences between rich and poor are central to the play.
- Birling jokes that the family need to **'behave ourselves, don't get into the police court or start a scandal'** *(Act One)* in order to secure the knighthood. His complacency is crucial here, as he has no idea what is about to be revealed about his **'nice'** family *(Act One)* and their relationship to Eva Smith. This is an example of **proleptic irony**.
- While Birling and Gerald laugh together, Eric re-enters and helps himself to more port. We learn later that Eric has a secret drink problem. This is an example of how Priestley builds the idea of hidden secrets into the play.

The fact that the Birlings drink port after dinner highlights their wealth and luxury lifestyle

- Birling's **hypocritical** views about personal responsibility – **'a man has to make his own way – has to look after himself'** *(Act One)* – are important as such views are inappropriate for a former Lord Mayor and future knight since both positions are associated with service to the community.

Episode 3 – Arrival of the Inspector

This section begins: **'EDNA: Please, sir, an inspector's called'** *(Act One).*

Edna, the **parlour maid**, announces the arrival of the Inspector. Mr Birling assumes the visit is linked to his job as a **magistrate**; Gerald jokes that Eric may have been **'up to something'** *(Act One)*, while Eric's uneasiness suggests a guilty secret. Inspector Goole begins his enquiries into a young woman's suicide, describing her agonizing death in graphic detail. He names the victim as Eva Smith and mentions that she left a diary, letter and photograph at her lodgings.

The Inspector shows the photograph to Birling to jog his memory but refuses to allow the other men to see it, insisting, **'One person and one line of inquiry at a time'** *(Act One)*.

- Almost the first words spoken by the Inspector are **'I'm on duty'** *(Act One)*, as he refuses Birling's invitation to take a drink; this phrase is significant as 'duty' and 'responsibility' are concepts that Priestley wishes to **foreground** in the play.
- Birling boasts of his high position in Brumley and his former titles of **alderman** and **Lord Mayor**, but the Inspector seems unimpressed. He is more concerned with an individual's conscience than he is with status – a key idea in the play.
- The Inspector uses 'shock tactics' in describing the young woman's death as he attempts to prick the conscience of each of his 'suspects' and make the audience imagine her suffering.

Key quotations

Burnt her inside out, of course. *(Inspector, Act One)*

Yes, she was in great agony. *(Inspector, Act One)*

alderman a senior member of a town council

foreground to focus on and bring to the attention of the audience

hypocrisy a form of insincerity; somebody who is hypocritical is a person whose actions are very different from his or her stated beliefs

Lord Mayor somebody elected to be head of local government in a large city

magistrate a person who acts as a judge in a magistrates' court, dealing with minor offences; magistrates are expected to be 'good and lawful'– capable of making thoughtful and fair decisions

parlour maids employed in private homes to wait on the family and their guests in the parlour (reception room); their responsibilities included setting and clearing the table, serving food and opening the door to guests

proleptic irony occurs when a character says something that turns out to be wrong or more significant than he or she thought at the time

Activity 2

Re-read the section of Act One from the entrance of the Inspector to the re-entrance of Sheila. Count how many times Birling avoids opportunities to express sympathy for Eva Smith's death or regret for his previous actions or decisions. What does this tell you about his character?

Episode 4 – Interrogation of Mr Birling

This section begins with Birling's admission that he recognizes Eva Smith: **'I seem to remember hearing that name – Eva Smith – somewhere'** *(Act One)*.

Birling's actions as an employer are scrutinized by the Inspector as he questions him about Eva Smith, whom Birling recognizes from the photograph. Eventually he admits to having sacked Eva from his factory for her part in a **strike** about pay. Despite hearing disturbing details about her suicide, Birling maintains he has done nothing wrong.

- Birling is complacent about his refusal to increase the workers' wages to **'twenty-five shillings a week'** *(Act One)*, then affronted when the Inspector asks, **'Why?'** *(Act One)*, unused to anyone, especially an 'inferior', questioning his actions; these are typical traits of his character.
- Gerald supports the sacking of Eva; while Eric describes it as **'tough luck'** *(Act One)*. Birling justifies his actions, saying: **'If you don't come down sharply on some of these people, they'd soon be asking for the earth'** *(Act One)*. This reveals his perceptions of class division.
- The Inspector's lack of **deference** towards Birling irritates him so he tries to intimidate the policeman, first by asking him to repeat his name (as if he were going to report him), and then referring to his golfing 'friend', the chief constable. The Inspector appears unshaken. Notions of rank, superiority, respect and 'due deference' are repeated throughout the play.
- Birling tries to shift the focus away from his own involvement with Eva's suicide to ask, **'what happened to her after that? Get into trouble? Go on the streets?'** *(Act One)*. Birling's use of **euphemism** and the casual nature of his questions betray complete lack of concern for his former employee – another example of his selfishness.

deference an expression of respect shown towards a person deemed to be superior in social rank, wealth or wisdom. In 1912, people like Mr and Mrs Birling expected their social inferiors – including police inspectors – to be deferential towards them

euphemism a word or phrase used in place of one that might be considered offensive or indelicate in good company

strike to stop working for a fixed or unlimited time to protest against low pay or unfair treatment

Activity 3

There are several euphemisms for prostitution in the play:

Go on the streets? *(Mr Birling, Act One)*

Now she had to try something else. *(Inspector, Act One)*

... she stopped being Eva Smith, looking for a job, and became Daisy Renton, with other ideas. *(Inspector, Act Two)*

women of the town *(Gerald, Act Two)*

What does the use of euphemisms suggest about the characters and their connection with Eva Smith? Does the Inspector's use of euphemism differ in any way from that of Birling and Gerald?

Episode 5 – Interrogation of Sheila

This section begins with Sheila's entry: **'SHEILA** ***[gaily]*****: What's this about streets?'** *(Act One).*

Despite Birling's best efforts to protect her from **'this unpleasant business'** *(Act One)*, when Sheila enters, the Inspector repeats the story of Eva Smith's suicide, stressing that she died **'after several hours of agony'** *(Act One)*. Sheila is genuinely distressed by the news.

- Sheila acknowledges her involvement in the events that lead to Eva's death and the sight of the photograph sends her sobbing from the room. Unlike Mr Birling, Sheila feels guilty about her actions, emphasizing the difference between the reactions of the younger and the older Birlings.

The Inspector questions Sheila, showing her the photograph, in the 1954 film

- Birling is angry with the Inspector and accuses him of ruining the **'nice little family celebration'** *(Act One)*, which highlights his indifference towards the dead girl. Priestley uses **juxtaposition** to contrast the comfortable lives that the Birlings enjoy with the harsh suffering that Eva had to endure. This emphasizes the effects of the social divides in the play as well as the prevailing attitudes of **complacency** and selfishness.

complacency a form of self-satisfaction or smugness

juxtaposition placing two images or ideas side-by-side to highlight the difference between them

Key quotations

INSPECTOR [*steadily*]: That's more or less what I was thinking earlier tonight, when I was in the Infirmary looking at what was left of Eva Smith. A nice little promising life there, I thought, and a nasty mess somebody's made of it. *(Act One)*

Episode 6 – Sheila's confession and suspicion

This section begins with Birling's exit: **'BIRLING...** ***goes out, closing door sharply behind him*'** *(Act One)*.

Birling exits to tell his wife what is happening. The Inspector, once again, refuses to allow Eric and Gerald to see the photograph. Sheila returns and confesses she'd had Eva sacked from Milwards for smiling behind her back as she tried on a garment that didn't suit her: **'I went to the manager and told him that this girl had been very impertinent'** *(Act One)*. Sheila recognizes her responsibility and feels remorse for what she did.

The Inspector's mention of the name Daisy Renton clearly startles Gerald and when Eric takes the Inspector out of the room, Sheila tries to make Gerald confess that he knew Daisy and was seeing her the previous summer.

- The Inspector has already mentioned a **'chain of events'** *(Act One)* leading to Eva's suicide and Gerald's reluctant admission that he knew Daisy indicates another link in the chain.
- Priestley increases the tension as the characters begin to realize the extent of the Inspector's knowledge. Sheila warns Gerald against trying to keep facts hidden from the Inspector: **'Why – you fool –** ***he knows*****. Of course he knows'** *(Act One)*.

Activity 4

1. Re-read the section where Sheila confesses how she got Eva the sack. Make a list of Sheila's motives for doing so.
2. How does Priestley choose to present Sheila at this point in the play? What does he reveal about her character?

Act Two

Episode 1 – Gerald's confession

This section begins with the opening of Act Two, as the Inspector begins to question Gerald: **'Well?'** *(Act Two)*.

Gerald asks the Inspector to excuse Sheila from hearing any more **'unpleasant and disturbing'** evidence *(Act Two)*, but Sheila insists on staying so that she will not feel solely responsible for the death of Eva Smith.

Mrs Birling enters with self-importance and Sheila tries, without success, to persuade her mother not to alienate the Inspector or to **'build up a kind of wall between us and that girl'** *(Act Two)*.

Mr Birling asks the Inspector to interview Eric immediately, so that he can go to bed, but the Inspector refuses, insisting that **'He must wait his turn'** *(Act Two)*.

Both Mr and Mrs Birling are shocked when the Inspector explains that Eva changed her name to **'Daisy Renton, with other ideas'** *(Act Two)* and then turns to Gerald to ask, **'when did you first get to know her?'** *(Act Two)*. Their illusions about Gerald are about to be shattered.

- Priestley increases the sense of mystery surrounding the Inspector's identity through the way Sheila reacts to him: she stares at him ***'wonderingly'*** *(Act Two)* and tells him **'I don't understand about you'** *(Act Two)*.
- Mrs Birling's reaction to the Inspector emphasizes the obstinacy of the older Birlings. She ignores Sheila's advice and deals with the Inspector as a social inferior, accusing him of impertinence and reminding him of her husband's importance in Brumley.

Tips for assessment

When considering the role of individual characters, remember to think about how their attitudes as well as their actions link them to the chain of events that led to Eva's death.

Episode 2 – Interrogation of Gerald

This section begins with Gerald's confession: **'All right, if you must have it. I met her first, some time in March last year...'** *(Act Two).*

Gerald explains how and where he met Daisy Renton and how he saved her from the clutches of Alderman Meggarty. He confesses to having set up Daisy as his mistress, thus solving the mystery of his whereabouts the previous summer when he **'never came near'** Sheila *(Act One).* Gerald leaves the Birlings' house to recover from the shock of Daisy's death.

- The description of the alderman's predatory attitude to women reinforces the idea that public office is no guarantee of good character, an idea that Priestley raises elsewhere in the play.
- Priestley suggests that Sheila has the capacity to learn from what has happened, when she states, **'You and I aren't the same people who sat down to dinner here'** *(Act Two).* This represents an important way in which certain characters develop during the course of the play.

Activity 5

Why do you think Priestley decided to include reference to Alderman Meggarty? What does it reveal about Gerald? Use quotations to support your view.

Episode 3 – Interrogation of Mrs Birling

This section begins with Gerald's departure as the Inspector turns his attention to Mrs Birling, who asks, **'You have a photograph of this girl?'** *(Act Two).*

The Inspector's direct manner of questioning infuriates Mr Birling, but Sheila begins to see him as a moral force, with the capability to educate the family about their responsibilities.

The Inspector reveals that Mrs Birling was the last member of the family to see Eva alive when, pregnant and desperate, she had turned to a Brumley charity – headed by Mrs Birling – for assistance. Mrs Birling defends her decision to reject the girl's appeal for help.

Eric is heard leaving the house early in the section and it ends with his return.

- Priestley draws attention to ideas of duty and responsibility through the repetition of associated words. It is notable that the Inspector and Mr and Mrs Birling use words like **'duty'** and **'responsibility'**, but appear to associate them with different values and priorities.
- Priestley presents Mr and Mrs Birling in unity in this section as they support one another's decisions. This perhaps reveals how easily unfair behaviour can be perpetuated and enforced when people in positions of privilege work together to impose their views.

Mrs Birling faces questioning in the 2009 National Theatre production

Key quotations

MRS BIRLING: I think it was simply a piece of gross impertinence – quite deliberate – and naturally that was one of the things that prejudiced me against her case.

BIRLING: And I should think so! Damned impudence! *(Act Two)*

Activity 6

Re-read the ending of Act Two, from Mrs Birling's line, **'Oh – a lot of silly nonsense!'** to Eric's return. How does Priestley build dramatic tension in this section?

Tips for assessment

Upgrade

When writing about Mrs Birling in your assessment, consider her use of language, such as her frequent use of negative and dismissive phrases. You should comment on how Priestley uses this technique to create a very distinct impression of her character.

Act Three

Episode 1 – Interrogation of Eric

This section begins with the opening of Act Three as the Inspector begins to question Eric: **'ERIC: You know, don't you?'** *(Act Three).*

Eric confesses to having met Eva in the Palace bar and later forcing his way into her lodgings. He admits that he made her pregnant and stole from the firm to support her. Eric confirms the story Eva told Mrs Birling about refusing both to marry him and to accept stolen money. He reacts violently to the news that Mrs Birling refused to help Eva.

The Inspector delivers a stark warning to the family about responsibility and the outlook for the future if people do not acknowledge their mutual responsibilities.

- Priestley presents Eric's conduct in this section as surprisingly honest and truthful. He returns to 'face the music'; suggesting that his outlook has changed since the beginning of the play.
- Angered to hear that his mother refused Eva assistance, Eric accuses her of having **'killed [...] my child – your own grandchild'** *(Act Three).* Unwittingly, Mrs Birling has destroyed a family member, reminding the audience ironically of Birling's earlier advice, **'to look after himself – and his family too'** *(Act One).*
- This section features the critical message of the play. The Inspector reminds the Birlings that they each had a part to play in Eva's suicide. The Inspector warns that unless people learn to take their responsibilties to others seriously **'they will be taught it in fire and blood and anguish'** *(Act Three).* The Inspector's tone shifts in these lines as he appears to speak prophetically about the future.

Episode 2 – The Inspector leaves

This section begins with the departure of the Inspector: ***'He walks straight out, leaving them staring, subdued and wondering'*** *(Act Three).*

As soon as the Inspector leaves, Birling blames Eric for destroying his chances of getting a knighthood. Mrs Birling also expresses outrage at Eric. Both are concerned about a **'public scandal'** *(Act Three),* while Eric and Sheila both appear to have been deeply affected by their role in Eva's death.

- Priestley highlights the Inspector's role as 'educator' in the play, by the way in which the characters react to his departure. Sheila accuses her parents of having learned nothing. Birling retorts that he has **'learnt plenty'** *(Act Three).*
- Priestley emphasizes the differences in attitude between the younger and older generation. Eric and Sheila believe that the family's guilt is all that matters. However, Mr and Mrs Birling see a possibility of a 'way out' from the consequences of their actions, if the Inspector was merely bluffing.

Activity 7

When the Inspector leaves, some of the characters mention the idea of 'learning' something from the Inspector's visit.

1. Re-read the Act up to this point and identify which characters refer to 'learning'.
2. Looking carefully at the phrases they use, divide the characters into those who are sincere in wishing to learn something from the events of the evening and those who are not. Explain your choices and include quotations.

Birling telephones his friend in an attempt to prove the Inspector is a hoaxer.

Episode 3 – The Inspector's identity

This section begins with the re-entrance of Gerald: **'I hope you don't mind my coming back?'** *(Act Three).*

Gerald returns and announces that there is no new police inspector in Brumley, which Birling confirms by ringing his chief constable friend. Believing the Inspector to be a hoaxer, the older Birlings and Gerald consider the possibility that their actions may not even relate to the same girl. Eric and Sheila are horrified by this development. Gerald even persuades the older Birlings that the whole story of the suicide may be part of the hoax and he rings the infirmary to check whether or not a girl has died.

When Gerald is told **'No girl has died in there today'** *(Act Three)*, Sheila and Eric refuse to be consoled. Mr Birling is triumphant, but then the telephone rings and his sense of victory is short-lived. He relays the message to the others that **'A girl has just died'** *(Act Three)* and that **'a police inspector is on his way here – to ask some – questions'** *(Act Three).*

- Priestley suggests that Birling's bluster about his standing in the community may be another empty truth as Birling accepts Gerald's theory about the hoax, stating: **'There are people in this town who dislike me enough to do that'** *(Act Three).* This once again raises the theme of secrets and lies.

- Gerald insists that **'Everything's all right now, Sheila'** *(Act Three)* and Birling encourages her to take back the engagement ring. Priestley uses this to suggest that Gerald and Birling are unlikely to reform their attitudes or behaviour, preferring simply to restore order.
- The phone rings to announce the imminent arrival of a police inspector – their ordeal is about to begin, all over again. This final twist in the plot is intended to shock the audience as much as it shocks the Birlings. By ending the play here, Priestley refuses to provide a neat conclusion, so that the audience is left thinking about the play long after the curtain has fallen.

Activity 8

Go back through the main points of the plot as outlined in this chapter. Identify what you believe to be the single most important 'event' for each Act. Compare your ideas with others in your class and discuss why you have selected your three chosen plot events.

Structure

Theatrical structure

In *An Inspector Calls*, Priestley draws on two familiar literary genres – the 'well-made play' and the 'whodunit' – as well as using some devices from classical Greek theatre. However, he does not follow any of these conventional structures slavishly.

The 'well-made play'

The key features of this genre are:

- a tightly constructed plot
- action based on events that have taken place before the opening of the play
- the building of suspense through a series of plot complications
- a climax near or at the end of the play where truths are uncovered or secrets revealed
- a happy ending.

The 'whodunit'

This genre often follows the structure of the well-made play but has these additional features:

- a murder or mystery to be solved
- a highly competent detective figure, investigating the murder and interrogating a range of suspects
- a series of clues to the identity of the murderer
- a climax, where the murderer is revealed and accepts guilt for the crime.

Priestley departs from both established genres in the following ways:

- each of the 'suspects' that Inspector Goole interrogates is guilty of contributing to the death of Eva Smith but only Sheila and Eric accept their responsibility
- the mystery element is not about who killed Eva Smith; it is about who or what the Inspector represents
- the 'happy ending' that the elder Birlings and Gerald begin to celebrate at the end of the play quickly turns sour when Birling answers the final telephone call.

Activity 9

1. Look through the first Act and identify clues that Priestley gives about Gerald's secret past and then do the same for Eric.
2. How does Priestley reveal these clues and how do they affect the audience's experience of the play?

Greek tragedy

Priestley chooses to tell his story in a three-act format with no formal scene divisions. He structures the play using some dramatic devices recognizable from Greek tragedy. Notably, he chooses to observe the three unities.

The Theatre of Dionysus (built 6th century BCE) where plays were performed to audiences in Ancient Greece

The three unities

Unity of time means that the playing time of the play follows precisely the amount of time that the action takes to unfold (therefore time does not elapse between the Acts).

Unity of place means that all the action happens in the same place – the Birling's dining room.

Unity of action means that there is only one plot (or one line of action).

By observing the three unities, Priestley must ensure that much of the 'action' that is reported in the play (the sacking of Eva, her dismissal from Milwards, her 'seduction' by Gerald and Eric, and her appearance before Mrs Birling's charity committee) occurs **off-stage**, as in Greek tragedy.

Activity 10

Why do you think Priestley decided to keep to the 'three unities'? What are the effects of this? You might consider how likely it is that every person at the dinner party in some way contributed to Eva's death.

Key facts about Greek tragedy

- The Ancient Greeks are generally considered to be the 'inventors' of drama, as we know it, in the Western World.
- A small number of the works of three major Greek playwrights, Aeschylus, Sophocles and Euripides (all writing in the 5th century BC), have survived. These plays reveal that the subject matter of Greek tragedy, though varied, always dealt with the relationship between human beings and the gods.
- In the 4th century BC, the Greek philosopher Aristotle wrote about the rules and conventions of Greek tragedy. Along with the works of the playwrights mentioned above, these writings have had a huge influence upon the development of world drama to this day.

Although the play is called *An Inspector Calls* and the Inspector is an important figure in the play, it is worth considering whether Priestley perhaps intends Birling to be seen as the main **protagonist**, with the Inspector fulfilling the function of the **antagonist**. In Greek tragedy, the protagonist usually begins with a good reputation before suffering a downfall because of a fatal flaw – usually pride or **hubris**. In *An Inspector Calls*, Birling's reputation and the prospect of his knighthood are threatened by his involvement in the scandal surrounding Eva Smith.

antagonist the character who opposes the lead character

hubris excessive pride that ultimately leads to a character's downfall

off-stage action that is referred to, or reported by, characters on-stage, but is not physically shown on stage; such as Eva's death

protagonist the main character

Activity 11

Who do you believe to be the 'main' character in the play? Find evidence to support your viewpoint.

A play of three acts

Priestley's play is divided into three acts. This structure is also influenced by Greek tragedy.

The structure of Act One

The opening of the Act is the **exposition** scene. The audience is introduced to the Birlings and witnesses their lavish lifestyle. Birling's smug self-satisfaction could be perceived as hubris or his fatal flaw. The Inspector interrupts the party and begins investigating the death of a young woman, one character at a time. This is part of the development of the action. The Act ends on a **cliff-hanger**, as the audience anticipates the Inspector's interrogation of Gerald.

The structure of Act Two

The action develops as two further characters are interviewed and their involvement with Eva is revealed. Tension builds towards the end of this Act as suspicion grows that Eric also played a part in Eva's death and the audience anticipates his return.

The structure of Act Three

Eric confesses his role in Eva's life and death, and succeeds in shocking Mrs Birling into a state of distressed recognition of what she has done. All of the family sense **catastrophe** about to engulf them. This is the **climax** of the action. The Inspector concludes that all of the family contributed to Eva's death and he urges them to learn the lesson about responsibility to others. He can be seen as Birling's **nemesis**.

catastrophe in Greek tragedy, the concluding part of the play when the protagonist accepts ruin

cliff-hanger the closing moments of a chapter, scene or episode that ends in suspense, creating anticipation about what will happen next

climax the highest or most intense part of the play or a turning point in the action; a feature of Greek tragedy

exposition key information to help the audience make sense of the play; a feature of Greek tragedy

nemesis in Greek tragedy, a person or force that inflicts punishment or revenge

Director Stephen Daldry chose to show Mr and Mrs Birling's ruin and downfall in the 2009 National Theatre production

In the third and final Act of the play Sheila and Eric experience 'tragic recognition' of their guilt, which the Greeks called **anagnorisis**. At this point the audience should experience tragic **catharsis**. However, Priestley suddenly **subverts** the tragic structure by apparently revealing that the agent of the family's ordeal is a 'hoaxer'.

As Gerald and the older Birlings review the events of the evening, they decide that they have simply been **'had, that's all'** *(Act Three)*. This lift in tone moves the play to an apparently safe resolution or **denouement**. The ringing telephone shatters that mood and the play ends on a reversal in fortune or **peripeteia**, as the characters realize that they must face further interrogation into their guilt.

anagnorisis the recognition of the error of one's ways; a feature of Greek tragedy

catharsis in Greek tragedy, an outrush of emotions as the audience sees the results of the tragedy played out – they pity the broken characters and think about how their actions relate to their own conduct

denouement resolution of the plot; a feature of Greek tragedy

peripeteia a reversal of fortunes just as escape or security had seemed possible; a feature of Greek tragedy

subvert to undermine or challenge expectations

Activity 12

How many features of Greek tragedy can you identify in *An Inspector Calls*? Choose three examples and, for each one, explain the effects Priestley creates by including this feature.

Dramatic structure

In addition to using the forms and conventions mentioned in the previous section, Priestley uses a variety of dramatic devices to shape the events and engage the audience's attention.

The Inspector's investigation provides a strong internal structure for the play as he proceeds to question each of the 'suspects', methodically, **'One person and one line of inquiry at a time'** *(Act One)*. He also tells Birling that what might have driven Eva Smith to suicide is **'A chain of events'** *(Act One)*. The **linear structure** of the play mirrors that chain, with each member of the Birling family (and Gerald) representing one of the links.

There is also a **circular structure** to the play in that it opens with the engagement and Sheila's delighted acceptance of her engagement ring and closes just after Gerald offers Sheila the ring for a second time, which she refuses, saying, **'No, not yet. It's too soon. I must think'** *(Act Three)*. The action of the play also appears to be about to begin again with the final line, **'a police inspector is on his way here – to ask some – questions'** *(Act Three)*.

Priestley structures each individual Act so that not all characters are present throughout; they come and go in a perfectly realistic way, allowing the Inspector to accumulate evidence for the audience which is not shared by all of the characters at any one time.

circular structure a narrative that ends more or less where it begins or which repeats moments of action from the beginning at the end

linear structure a straightforward, chronological narrative that has a beginning, middle and an end – in that order

Activity 13

Look at the episodes identified in the Plot section. Draw up a table to show which characters are on stage for each episode, including who enters the stage and who leaves the stage during this time. Use colour coding to highlight different characters to help you to see the 'traffic' on stage. Do you notice anything interesting?

Writing about plot and structure

Upgrade

In your assessment you are likely to have the opportunity to show what you know about the significance of specific aspects of plot. You may also be asked to comment on the structure of the play and how Priestley reveals aspects of plot through the device of the Inspector's interrogation. Always make sure that you answer the precise focus of the question and never simply tell the story of the play.

Biography of J.B. Priestley

J.B. Priestley, playwright, radio broadcaster and socialist (1894–1984)

- John Priestley was born in Bradford in 1894. His mother was a former mill worker and his father was a schoolmaster who inspired him to develop a social conscience.
- He wrote a regular column (unpaid) for *The Bradford Pioneer*, where he aired his opinions on topics such as music and film, as well as arguing against the imminent war.
- The First World War (1914–18) had a huge impact on him. He volunteered for the army in 1914 and served on the Western Front where some of the most appalling loss of life occurred.
- Although many of his friends were killed in action, Priestley survived injury. He emerged from his experience with deep loathing of the class system which, in war time, expressed itself in the gulf between officers and ordinary soldiers.
- Priestley studied Modern History and Political Science at Cambridge and wrote extensively on social issues and about the plight of the poor and unemployed.
- Among over 40 plays that Priestley wrote during his lifetime are his so-called 'time' plays: *Dangerous Corner* (1932), *Time and the Conways* (1937), *I Have Been Here Before* (1937) and *An Inspector Calls* (1945). In these plays, Priestley explores various contemporary theories about time.
- Priestley became a popular public figure; he strongly supported the formation of the **United Nations** as well as the **National Health Service**. Throughout his life he was a strong believer in the importance of shared social responsibility.
- Although Priestley declined the offer of a knighthood and a peerage, he accepted the Order of Merit in 1977, which was awarded personally by the Queen. He died in 1984.

National Health Service introduced by the Labour government in 1948, providing free medical care for all British citizens. Previously, patients had to pay privately for health care even though a large proportion of the population was too poor to afford it

United Nations a multi-national committee founded in 1945, following the Second World War, with the aim of preventing further wars between countries and offering a forum for discussion between all the nations of the world

Activity 1

Re-read the biographical points about Priestley's life. Which aspects of his life appear to have influenced the writing of *An Inspector Calls*? Refer to evidence from the play to support your ideas.

Historical and cultural context

The historical setting

Priestley wrote *An Inspector Calls* in 1945 for a post-war audience. However, the action of the play is set on a spring evening in 1912. The contrast between the way people lived in 1912 and the way they lived in 1945 was crucial in creating the effects that Priestley wanted to achieve. The context of the play is, therefore, the close of the Edwardian era, as seen from a post-Second World War **perspective**.

The action of the play is located in a fictional industrial city in the North Midlands that Priestley calls Brumley. However, as the entire play takes place in the Birling's formal dining room and the audience sees only wealthy characters (plus the Inspector) the regional, urban setting is only important in helping the audience to imagine the slum-like conditions that early 20th-century workers and the unemployed might have had to live in.

perspective a point of view; here of someone who has lived through two world wars and is facing the political realities of life in 1945

Wealthy Edwardians ate dinner in lavish style

In the 33 years between 1912 and 1945, British society changed significantly. Perhaps the most significant changes were brought about by the two world wars, which caused millions of deaths and injuries to British servicemen and women, as well as to countless civilians. One outcome of this shared experience of war was a change in attitudes towards the class system, which was so dominant in Edwardian society in the years leading up to the conflict. The system of **hierarchy** and social privilege was no longer accepted as the only possible structure for society.

The face of industry was also transformed by the increasing numbers of women in the workforce and the formation of trade unions, which gave the employee more power to negotiate fair pay and better working conditions.

The main purpose for setting *An Inspector Calls* in 1912 is to allow the audience to see just how wrong-headed Birling is in his predictions for the future. The fact that he is so blinkered about the times that he lives in suggests that his judgement is not to be trusted in other areas.

The 1945 audience would appreciate the folly of Birling's pronouncement that in 1940 **'these silly little war scares'** *(Act One)* will have been forgotten. All audiences also know how wrong he is about the **'unsinkable'** *Titanic (Act One)*.

Activity 2

Imagine you have been asked to bring *An Inspector Calls* up-to-date for a modern audience.

1. Think of two or three major world events that have occurred in recent history that someone as blinkered and self-centred as Birling might not have foreseen at the beginning of the year 2000.
2. How does this help you to see Birling as Priestley intended?

Social class

At the beginning of the 20th century, society was divided, unequally, into recognizable classes. Although a simplification, it is possible to see the class system as a pyramid, with royalty at the top and the working classes near the bottom, just above **vagrants** and the homeless.

hierarchy a system of putting people into ranks, with some having superiority and authority over others

vagrant a tramp, with no home and no work

The diagram on the next page shows the class system at the beginning of the 20th century.

Royalty

Aristocracy
People who originally received land or titles from the monarch and have passed them down through generations.

Upper class
People with high standing in the Church, Law, Military or Medicine. Also includes knights created by royalty or the government for services to the state.

Upper-middle class
Includes lower-ranking professionals with university educations and wealthy businessmen employing large numbers of workers.

Lower-middle class
Includes people with administrative or secretarial roles.

Working class
Includes shop workers and medical staff such as nurses.

Labouring class
Includes workers in mines, mills, factories and farms, doing gruelling or repetitive work for low pay.

Vagrant class
Includes the homeless, prostitutes and petty criminals.

Activity 3

1. Decide where each of the following characters from the play would fit into the class pyramid:

   a) Gerald Croft
   b) the Inspector
   c) Mr Birling
   d) Mrs Birling
   e) Sheila Birling
   f) Eva Smith.

2. Try to draw up a class pyramid for the 21st century. What are the major differences between your modern day structure and the social hierarchy shown above?

Birling is presented as a successful and wealthy industrialist. By marrying a woman who is his social superior, he has elevated himself a little further. We learn that Gerald's mother Lady Croft, comes from **'an old country family – landed people and so forth'** *(Act One)*, which is one of the reasons why Birling is so pleased with his future son-in-law. It also explains why he is anxious to be granted a knighthood, to help the family a little further up the social ladder.

Mr Birling's sensitivity about his social class, coupled with Mrs Birling's insistence on appropriate manners and behaviour, reflects the importance of the class structure in 1912. The fact that the Crofts do not attend the engagement party, merely sending **'a very nice cable'** *(Act One)*, suggests, as Birling privately admits, that they feel that Gerald **'might have done better'** for himself, **'socially'** *(Act One)*.

While the Birlings are acutely aware of their lower social status in relation to the Crofts, they are, nevertheless, very comfortable with displaying their superiority over others. Birling is keen to impress upon the Inspector, even before the investigation begins, that he has been **'an alderman for years – and Lord Mayor two years ago'** and that he is **'still on the Bench'** *(Act One)*, in order to demonstrate his superiority over ordinary citizens.

on the Bench refers to being a magistrate in a magistrates' court or, as it was called in 1912, the police court

Birling also shows contempt for his workforce, not only in the way he treats them in, for example, refusing to consider their request for higher wages, but also in the way he speaks about his employees. Priestley demonstrates a clear 'them and us' mentality in Birling's attitudes: **'if you don't come down sharply on some of these people, they'd soon be asking for the earth'** *(Act One)*. Gerald is just as disparaging when he comments on the workers' strike, observing, **'if it was just after the holidays. They'd be all broke – if I know them'** *(Act One)*.

Activity 4

Look again at the way Mr Birling speaks about his workforce in Act One.

1. Make a list of all the words that he uses to describe Eva and the rest of his workers. What does this reveal about Birling's character?
2. How do you think Priestley regards Mr Birling? Use evidence to support your views.

Mrs Birling is especially contemptuous of the lower classes, almost seeming to view them as a separate species. She suggests that she doesn't suppose **'for a moment that we can understand why the girl committed suicide'** *(Act Two)*, referring to Eva as one of the **'Girls of that class'** *(Act Two)*. She also admits that she decided to block Eva's appeal for assistance partly because Eva appeared to be **'claiming elaborate fine feelings and scruples that were simply absurd in a girl in her position'** *(Act One)*.

The character most acutely aware of social distinction is Mrs Birling. Meticulous in her observance of **etiquette**, she criticizes her husband for a lapse of manners and is shocked by Sheila's use of slang. Later in the play, she is outraged by the Inspector's **'impertinent'** manner of conducting his inquiry *(Act Two)*.

Activity 5

1. Why do you think Priestley emphasizes in his opening stage directions the fact that Mrs Birling is ***'her husband's social superior'***? How do you think Mrs Birling's 'superiority' is likely to affect the audience's view of Mr Birling?
2. Imagine you are performing the role of Mrs Birling on stage. How would you signal your superiority to the audience in your acting? Try acting out the opening of Act One to show this.

In contrast to Gerald Croft and the Birlings, the Inspector appears to be a **champion of the poor** and one of his main functions in the play is to teach the Birlings (and therefore the audience) some compassion for their fellow human beings, of whatever class. Early on in the investigation he tells Sheila, **'it would do us all a bit of good if sometimes we tried to put ourselves in the place of these young women counting their pennies in their dingy little back bedrooms'** *(Act One)*.

Although the Inspector is speaking in 1912, the audience he was addressing belonged to 1945 and his words act as Priestley's warning to them not to allow the old class divisions to blight the prospect of greater equality in the post-war nation.

champion of the poor a supporter of the poor

etiquette the rules about what is considered to be 'good manners' within polite sections of society

It would be wrong to suggest that the class system of the early 20th century no longer existed by 1945. However, the rigid structure had been eroded over the years, especially immediately after the Second World War when there was a great feeling of solidarity within a population that had been united against a common enemy.

Political change

In the first post-war general election in 1945, the Labour Party benefited from a boost in popularity and was voted into power as the Conservative Party, represented by Winston Churchill, was voted out. Voters were influenced by the expectation that the Labour Party would adopt ideas for **social reform** that had been put forward by William Beveridge. The Beveridge Report, published in 1942, formed the basis for a **manifesto for change** that would ensure better housing, free medical treatment and employment for all.

Far from being a period where, as Birling predicts in Act One, **'the interests of Capital – are properly protected'** *(Act One)*, when Priestley wrote the play it was obvious that it was the rights of 'Labour' that would be the chief concern of the new government. Audiences of the time would see Birling's self-assurance as misguided; modern audiences can also see the short-sightedness of Birling's confident pronouncements.

manifesto for change a published statement outlining political plans for change (in this case, improving living conditions for the majority of citizens)

social reform changes to improve the conditions in which people live and work

Activity 6

Carry out some research into the Beveridge Report and create a list of ten key points about it. This will help you to gain a clear idea of the social context of the play's first audiences.

Exploitation of workers

Linked to the class issue is Priestley's depiction of the ways in which the lower classes were exploited by their employers.

Eva Smith is, of course, the main representative of the exploited worker. Despite being a **'good worker'** *(Act One)* who was about to be promoted to **'a leading operator'** *(Act One)*, Eva was sacked from Birling and Company for being a ring-leader **'who'd started the trouble'** *(Act One)* that led to the strike. Significantly, at a time when female employees had no voice or representation in the workforce, Birling criticizes Eva for having **'a lot to say – far too much'** and he concludes **'so she had to go'** *(Act One)*.

In 1912, the cheapest labour available to industrialists like Sir George Croft and Arthur Birling would have been women. Priestley does not consider it necessary to specify what was made in the Birling 'works' (possibly something related to textiles, given the large number of women employed) but he is very specific about what the workers earned – they were **'averaging about twenty-two and six'** *(Act One)* per week.

In 1912, women worked 12-hour shifts in mills and factories for wages that barely covered the cost of living

Key quotations

There are a lot of young women living that sort of existence in every city and big town in this country, Miss Birling. If there weren't, the factories and warehouses wouldn't know where to look for cheap labour. Ask your father. *(Inspector, Act One)*

...she hadn't been able to save much out of what Birling and Company had paid her... *(Inspector, Act One)*

Activity 7

1. Research the price of food, drink and clothing in 1912. You will find plenty of information on the Internet. For example, a lady's hat, such as Mrs Birling might have been wearing when she turned down Eva Smith's appeal for assistance, would have cost more than thirty shillings.
2. What could a director do in a production to emphasize the vast difference in wealth between Eva and the Birlings?

Tips for assessment

When writing about the context of the play in your assessment, remember to show your knowledge of the key differences between Britain in 1912 and in 1945.

Priestley was a critic of the social hierarchies of capitalist society

In addition to employing women in his factory, Mr Birling, in common with all wealthy householders, would have employed domestic staff to run the home. The Birlings employ Edna, the parlour maid – a character who we see – and we know they keep a cook, **'Good dinner, too, Sybil. Tell cook from me'** *(Act One)*. This was perfectly normal for families like the Birlings in 1912. Nevertheless, Priestley suggests that Edna is being exploited when Mrs Birling assumes in Act Three that, however late, Edna will answer the door, adding, **'I asked her to wait up to make us some tea'** *(Act Three)*, emphasizing the fact that the Birlings always put their own comfort before the welfare of their domestic staff.

National Theatre production

In Stephen Daldry's ground-breaking production of *An Inspector Calls* for the National Theatre in 2009, Edna is seen enjoying the family's unease as she watches from outside the house while the Inspector makes each family member reveal their dishonourable actions.

Activity 8

Imagine you are in charge of casting a production of *An Inspector Calls*.

1. Write a paragraph describing the qualities you are looking for in the actress you want to play the role of Edna.
2. Add a second paragraph explaining why this small role is an important one in terms of Priestley's social message.

The position of women in society

Eva Smith is portrayed as a victim of exploitation stemming from her class and her gender. She is exploited by Mr Birling in her work and she is exploited sexually by both Gerald and Eric because of her 'inferiority' as a lower-class woman in Edwardian society.

Key quotations

She was out of work for the next two months. Both her parents were dead, so that she'd no home to go back to. And she hadn't been able to save much out of what Birling and Company had paid her. So that after two months, with no work, no money coming in, and living in lodgings, with no relatives to help her, few friends, lonely, half-starved, she was feeling desperate. *(Inspector, Act One)*

Both Mrs Birling and her daughter Sheila belong to a class of woman who would never expect to have to work to provide for themselves. Each would have known, while they were growing up, that they were destined to marry someone wealthy enough to provide a very comfortable lifestyle for them.

Girls born into upper- and middle-class families received an education that prepared them to become good wives and accomplished 'ornaments' in their husbands' homes. Their biggest responsibility lay in managing their staff of domestic servants. When such young women failed to find a suitable husband, they remained in the parental home and continued to be supported by their fathers.

Activity 9

Re-read the Inspector's description of Eva's situation in the key quotation above.

1. Rewrite the description to describe Sheila's position at the beginning of the play, echoing the same pattern of sentences and phrases that the Inspector uses. Your final sentence should end, 'she was feeling contented'.
2. What effects does Priestley achieve through contrasting Sheila's easy life with Eva's hard one?

During the Edwardian period, the majority of women who had to work went into service as maids, cooks or laundrywomen. Others, like Eva Smith, worked in factories or 'sweat-shops', toiling away day after day for a miserable wage. When Eva became 'Daisy Renton' she joined the ranks of thousands of women who were desperate enough to turn to prostitution to survive. This is when Gerald discovers her at the Palace music hall bar, which he describes as **'a favourite haunt of women of the town'** *(Act Two)*.

Women's position in society had changed significantly by the time Priestley wrote the play. Although equality was still a long way off, there were more opportunities for women in the workplace. Although there were still callous and selfish people, willing to exploit their fellow human beings, there would have been less reason for a parentless girl in 1945 to have reached the depths of despair that Eva did in 1912.

Prostitutes waiting for clients in a bar in the early 1900s

Activity 10

Go back through Act One and make a list of all the references you can find that show the Birlings' careless attitudes towards the exploitation of their fellow human beings.

Dramatic context

Around the time that Priestley was writing, drama in Britain was largely aimed at the upper and middle classes, who had both the money and the leisure time to enjoy a night at the theatre.

After the First World War, there were, unsurprisingly, a number of serious plays written that took war as a major theme. The most enduring of these was R.C. Sherriff's harrowing *Journey's End* (1928), written in a realistic style, and attracting much praise for its accurate portrayal of life and death in the trenches at the Western Front.

The light-hearted comedies of Noël Coward were also popular during this time; for example, *Private Lives* (1931) and *Blithe Spirit* (1941). Both plays deal with the complicated marital relationships of the upper-middle classes, where the comedy is based on improbable situations and witty dialogue.

In the 1930s and 1940s, a number of socialist theatre companies began to create drama to appeal to the working classes. For example, companies such as the 'Unity Theatre', 'The Red Megaphone' and 'Theatre of Action' had a socialist political agenda and used to take their drama to the streets or to the factory gates with the intention of promoting socialist ideas.

Activity 11

Using the Internet, find out about theatre audiences in the first half of the 20th century. How do you think the audience of 1945 would have responded to Priestley's message about the right of all people to be treated fairly and with respect? Give reasons to support your ideas.

Priestley's dramatic style

Priestley's most successful plays were not considered controversial in terms of their dramatic form. Most took place in largely domestic settings and were presented in a realistic style. While Priestley did experiment with dramatic form, bringing together music, ballet and masked characters in his 1939 play *Johnson over Jordan*, it was not a commercial success.

He returned to a more conventional dramatic style with *An Inspector Calls*. The play uses traditional features, which reflect other plays of the time and also hark back to Ancient Greek drama.

Activity 12

Write down ideas and then discuss the following question as a class:

Why do you think Priestley chose to use a traditional dramatic style for *An Inspector Calls*?

Think about:

- Priestley's 'message'
- audience appeal
- the events of the play
- any other reasons you can think of.

Writing about context

Upgrade

In order to show an understanding of the historical and cultural contexts surrounding the play, you need to be able to distinguish between what life was like in 1912 (when the play is set) and what life was like in 1945 (when the play was first performed). This understanding will help you to write effectively about:

- the significance of the setting
- how Priestley presents the roles and relationships of each of the characters
- the language of the play, especially the formal language of Mrs Birling and the more 'modern' slang used by the younger generation
- Priestley's attitudes and techniques, especially with regards to the presentation of particular themes in the play
- the play's relevance today.

Main characters

The main characters in this play are Mr and Mrs Birling, Sheila and Eric, Gerald Croft and Inspector Goole. Edna, the parlour maid, plays a very small part. Although Eva Smith never appears, she is central to the play.

The following diagram shows how each character relates to Eva Smith.

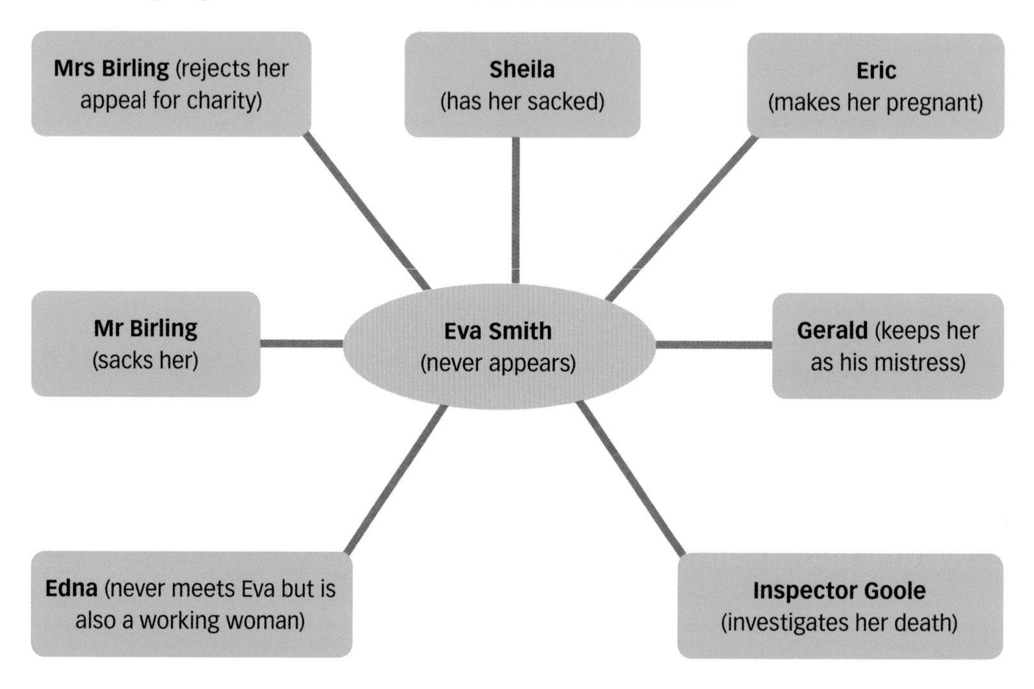

Mr Arthur Birling

Priestley describes Arthur Birling in the opening stage directions of Act One.

Key quotations

ARTHUR BIRLING *is a heavy-looking, rather portentous man in his middle fifties with fairly easy manners but rather provincial in his speech.* (Act One)

In the first Act, Birling appears as a successful self-made businessman whose 'friendly' rivalry with Crofts Limited is on the brink of being transformed into a more cooperative relationship, thanks to the engagement of Gerald and Sheila. Birling is *'pleased' (Act One)* with himself, to begin with, although his self-satisfied attitude takes a few knocks over the course of the play.

Priestley uses Birling to represent capitalist attitudes. He gives Birling a platform for airing his opinions in Act One, when he delivers a toast to the couple. In this speech, and in his later pieces of 'advice' to Gerald and Eric, Birling shows himself to be overconfident and misguided in his views. For example, he describes the current fear of imminent war as **'fiddlesticks'** *(Act One).*

Activity 1

Re-read Mr Birling's 'speeches' to his family before the arrival of the Inspector in Act One. Make a list of all the opinions that he expresses. Do you agree with any of his views? Give reasons.

Birling is contemptuous of those whom he describes as **'cranks'** who believe **'everybody has to look after everybody else, as if we were all mixed up together like bees in a hive – community and all that nonsense'** *(Act One).* He insists on an 'every man for himself' approach to life, which is the polar opposite of the Inspector, who believes, **'We are members of one body. We are responsible for each other'** *(Act Three).*

When the Inspector arrives, Birling makes sure that he recognizes his high social standing as a long-term alderman, former Lord Mayor and serving magistrate. Rank is very important to Birling, as has already been seen in his attitude towards Lady Croft and his determination to receive a knighthood.

Activity 2

In groups of three, each looking at a different Act, find examples of occasions where Priestley presents Birling as unfit to be a magistrate. Look again at the definition of a magistrate's responsibilities on page 8. Make notes and share your ideas with your group.

Tips for assessment

Unlike a novelist, who can describe or comment directly on characters to help the reader understand them, a playwright must convey each 'personality' through dialogue or monologue that is then spoken by actors on the stage. In your assessment, you'll need to show how Priestley presents his characters through what they say and how they say it.

Priestley presents Mr Birling as an unimaginative and **unsympathetic character**. When confronted with the suicide of Eva Smith, Birling appears blind to the possibility that by sacking her he might have been responsible for setting Eva on a downward spiral to her death.

unsympathetic character a character who makes a negative impression on the audience

Key quotations

Look – there's nothing mysterious – or scandalous – about this business – at least not so far as I'm concerned. It's a perfectly straightforward case, and as it happened more than eighteen months ago – nearly two years ago – obviously it has nothing whatever to do with the wretched girl's suicide. Eh, Inspector? *(Mr Birling, Act One)*

Mr and Mrs Birling in the 2009 National Theatre production

Birling shows no sympathy for Eva Smith at any point. As the Inspector draws his investigation to a close, he reminds Birling that, although each of the Birlings **'helped to kill'** Eva *(Act Three)*, it was he who **'started it'** *(Act Three)* and all because she wanted a pitiful **'twenty-five shillings a week'** *(Act Three)*. At this stage, with his knighthood appearing to be jeopardized by imminent scandal, we see a change in Birling as he ***'unhappily'*** *(Act Three)* tells the Inspector **'I'd give thousands – yes, thousands'** *(Act Three)*, but the offer is too late and the audience can see that it is a gesture born out of self-pity rather than any true feeling for the girl.

Birling is in a state of shock when the Inspector leaves but he soon recovers enough to tell Eric, **'You're the one I blame for this'** *(Act Three)*. Priestley uses the disapproval of the younger generation to highlight Birling's selfishness as they look back on the events of the evening.

Key quotations

The point is, you don't seem to have learnt anything.
(Sheila to Mr Birling, Act Three)

Activity 3

Look again at the section of Act Three following the departure of the Inspector.

1. Pick out some examples of the differences between Mr Birling's reaction to the evening's events and the reactions of Sheila and Eric.
2. Why do you think Priestley decided to create a contrast between the ideas of the older and the younger characters in this part of the play?

Once Gerald has telephoned the infirmary and established that not only does the Inspector appear to be a hoaxer but that **'No girl has died in there today'** *(Act Three)*, Birling is ecstatic. When Sheila and Eric fail to share his sense of relief, he mocks them for their lack of a sense of humour. His euphoria turns to horror when he takes the final telephone call and realizes that the evening's ordeal is about to begin all over again.

Mr Birling is associated with themes of power and privilege, responsibility and duty as well as the themes of money and class.

Activity 4

Look closely at Mr Birling's advice to the two young men in Act One:

Key quotations

But this is the point. I don't want to lecture you two young fellows again. But what so many of you don't seem to understand now, when things are so much easier, is that a man has to make his own way – has to look after himself – and his family too, of course, when he has one – and so long as he does that he won't come to much harm. But the way some of these cranks talk and write now, you'd think everybody has to look after everybody else, as if we were all mixed up together like bees in a hive – community and all that nonsense. But take my word for it, you youngsters – and I've learnt in the good hard school of experience – that a man has to mind his own business and look after himself and his own...

Write a paragraph explaining how Priestley conveys Birling's character through his use of language and sentence structure.

Mrs Sybil Birling

Mrs Birling is presented as a snobbish and unfeeling woman, who is quick to criticize the behaviour of her own family as well as to judge Eva Smith's claims on her charity as fraudulent. We are also told she is Mr Birling's **'social superior'** *(Act One)* and this is emphasized in both her words and reported actions. She seems to look down on everybody apart from Gerald Croft.

In Act One almost all of her, relatively few, lines involve expressions of disapproval or rebuke.

Key quotations

Arthur, you're not supposed to say such things – *(Mrs Birling to Mr Birling, Act One)*

What an expression, Sheila! Really, the things you girls pick up these days! *(Mrs Birling, Act One)*

Now stop it, you two. *(Mrs Birling to Sheila and Eric, Act One)*

Now, Arthur, I don't think you ought to talk business on an occasion like this. *(Mrs Birling, Act One)*

Now, Sheila, don't tease him. *(Mrs Birling, Act One)*

Throughout the play, Mrs Birling treats her grown-up son and daughter like young children, referring to Eric as being in **'an excitable silly mood'** *(Act Two)* when he is actually drunk, and protesting that he is **'only a boy'** *(Act Two)* when the Inspector asks if Eric is used to drinking. She refers to Sheila as being **'Over-excited'** *(Act Two)* by the Inspector's inquiry and tries to hurry her off to bed, **'You'll feel better in the morning'** *(Act Two)*.

Priestley seems to suggest that Mrs Birling is the kind of woman that Sheila might have become, had she not encountered the Inspector. Neither Mr nor Mrs Birling appears to have provided a good role model for their children as they are both motivated by pride and self-interest.

Throughout the play Mrs Birling remains impervious to the idea that she might have been in the wrong in her dealings with Eva Smith. More significantly, she shows herself to be without any feelings of compassion for the suffering of Eva Smith, or any other **'Girls of that class'** *(Act Two)*, even after having discovered her own part in Eva's sorry story. The fact that a woman so lacking in charity should be leading the Brumley Women's Charity Organization is one of Priestley's greatest ironies in the play.

Activity 5

Look again at Act Two. Pick out all the negative points that Mrs Birling makes about Eva.

Key quotations

I'm sorry she should have come to such a horrible end. But I accept no blame for it at all. *(Mrs Birling, Act Two)*

...I did nothing I'm ashamed of or that won't bear investigation. *(Mrs Birling, Act Two)*

...I've done nothing wrong – and you know it. *(Mrs Birling, Act Two)*

Activity 6

Of all the characters questioned by the Inspector, Mrs Birling is the most hostile. Look closely at Mrs Birling's reaction to the Inspector below:

Key quotations

If you think you can bring any pressure to bear upon me, Inspector, you're quite mistaken. Unlike the other three, I did nothing I'm ashamed of or that won't bear investigation. The girl asked for assistance. We are asked to look carefully into the claims made upon us. I wasn't satisfied with this girl's claim – she seemed to me to be not a good case – and so I used my influence to have it refused. And in spite of what's happened to the girl since, I consider I did my duty. So if I prefer not to discuss it any farther, you have no power to make me change my mind. *(Mrs Birling, Act Two)*

Paying close attention to Priestley's use of vocabulary and sentence structure, explain the impression you get of Mrs Birling's character from this extract.

Mrs Birling resists the Inspector's attempts to stir her conscience. Although finally appalled to realize that Eric is the father of Eva's unborn child, Mrs Birling appears more shocked by the fact that Eric **'stole money'** *(Act Three)*. She does, however, become distressed when Eric turns on her, ***'almost threatening her'*** *(Act Three)*, and accuses her of killing Eva **'and the child she'd have had, too – my child – your own grandchild'** *(Act Three)*.

Mrs Birling's distress does not last long and as soon as Gerald confirms that the Inspector wasn't **'a police officer'** *(Act Three)* she reverts to her previous complacency, boasting: **'I was the only one of you who didn't give in to him'** *(Act Three)* and strenuously attempting to prevent Gerald from learning about the other 'skeletons' that have 'come out of the cupboard' since he left the house.

Activity 7

1. Do you believe the Inspector is right when he tells Mrs Birling that she will spend the rest of her life regretting her actions towards Eva? Why/Why not?
2. Do you think the Inspector is at all successful in encouraging Mrs Birling to reflect on her actions? Use evidence from the text to support your ideas.
3. Why do you think Priestley decided to present the Inspector's dealings with Mrs Birling as a 'failure'?

Sybil Birling is linked to themes of power and responsibility, social inequality, charity and family, shame and blame, secrets and lies.

Sheila Birling

Sheila is presented as a **sympathetic character**. Although we discover that her bad temper and jealousy resulted in Eva being dismissed from Milwards, Sheila is deeply ashamed of her actions. Once confronted with the consequences, she never recovers from her guilt.

Sheila represents the younger generation and some prospect of hope for the future. When Mrs Birling tells the Inspector, **'You seem to have made a great impression on this child, Inspector'** *(Act Two)*, he replies, **'We often do on the young ones. They're more impressionable'** *(Act Two)*, suggesting that young people like Sheila (and Eric) are open to change.

Sheila's reaction to the description of Eva's suffering is spontaneous sympathy; she asks the Inspector if Eva was young and if she was pretty – looking for points of comparison with her own life. At this stage she has no idea that she and Eva have more in common than youth and good looks; in fact, they have each shared the affections of Gerald Croft.

One of Sheila's functions in the play, in addition to her contribution to the death of Eva, is to alert the audience to the very different circumstances that Sheila Birling and Eva Smith have experienced. She therefore acts as a **foil** to Eva Smith, helping Priestley to illustrate the evils of the class system.

foil a character whose function is to serve as a contrast to another character

sympathetic character a character that the audience can identify with and that therefore makes a positive impression

Activity 8

Write down all of the ways that Sheila Birling's life differs from that of Eva Smith.

Sheila Birling in the 2009 National Theatre production

Despite her role in Eva's destruction, Sheila is shown to have a social conscience. She recognizes that working-class girls are not just **'cheap labour – they're *people*'** *(Act One)*. She also consistently comments on the unfolding events of the play, in a way that shows that she shares the Inspector's views about her family's collective responsibility for Eva's death and the terrible injustice of their actions.

Key quotations

I think it was a mean thing to do. Perhaps that spoilt everything for her. *(Sheila, Act One)*

It's a rotten shame. *(Sheila, Act One)*

Mother, I think it was cruel and vile. *(Sheila, Act Two)*

Priestley uses Sheila's thoughtful response to the Inspector and his apparent powers to steer the audience towards viewing him as some sort of super-human force with superior knowledge and a special mission to educate the Birlings.

Key quotations

Why – you fool – *he knows*. Of course he knows. And I hate to think how much he knows that we don't know yet. You'll see. You'll see. *(Sheila, Act One)*

I have an idea – and I had it all along vaguely – that there was something curious about him. He never seemed like an ordinary police inspector – *(Sheila, Act Three)*

Sheila learns about herself as a result of the visit of the Inspector and does not feel relieved by the disclosure that Inspector Goole was not a police officer, nor does the news that **'No girl has died'** *(Act Three)* in the infirmary alter her sense of guilt.

Sheila is linked to themes of responsibility, truth and personal growth.

Activity 9

1. Discuss the following questions:
   a. How would you summarize Sheila's development in the play?
   b. Do you think the Inspector achieves what he set out to achieve by encouraging Sheila to change, even if the older members of her family remain set in their ways?
2. Write two paragraphs in answer to each question, using evidence from the text to support your points.

Eric Birling

Although Eric Birling is not a particularly sympathetic character initially, like Sheila, he is deeply affected by the Inspector's revelations. In Act One, Eric and Sheila squabble like children, but the guilt that they share over Eva's death brings them closer together and they both grow up over the course of the play.

Neither Mr nor Mrs Birling treats Eric as an adult. Mrs Birling scolds him in varying degrees of severity throughout the play while Mr Birling seems determined not to listen to a word he says.

Sheila and Eric both accept their guilt at the end of the play

Key quotations

Silly boy! Where can he have gone to? *(Mrs Birling, Act Two)*

Why, you hysterical young fool – get back – or I'll – *(Mr Birling, Act Three)*

Activity 10

In the stage directions, Priestley describes Eric as **'not quite at ease, half shy, half assertive'** *(Act One)*. Create a sketch or spider diagram with notes about how, in your opinion, Eric should be presented on stage.

a. Provide some general guidance on how the actor should portray Eric's movements on stage, based on what you know about him from the text.

b. Select three lines from the play that reveal something about Eric's character. For each line that you have chosen, give brief instructions on how you think an actor should deliver the lines – based on what you know about Eric's character.

When Sheila remarks, early on in the play, that Eric is **'squiffy'** *(Act One)* she draws the audience's attention to his drinking problem. Eric is revealed as a young man who **'drink[s] far too much'** *(Act Two)* possibly as an outlet for his frustration which is both personal – his parents still treat him like a child – and professional – he is apparently not living up to Mr Birling's expectations at work.

Activity 11

Why do you think Priestley decided to show that Eric has a drinking problem in the play? Write three paragraphs in answer to this question, including references to the text. Think about:

- what impact it is likely to have on the audience's reaction to Eric
- what it reveals about Mr and Mrs Birling
- how it links with other themes in the play.

Although Eric is guilty of irresponsibly fathering a child with a woman he had no intention of marrying, Priestley also seems keen to show that, ultimately, he has more of a social conscience than Gerald and either of his parents. For example, Eric appears to understand the plight of Birling's underpaid workforce.

Key quotations

Why shouldn't they try for higher wages? We try for the highest possible prices. And I don't see why she should have been sacked just because she'd a bit more spirit than the others. You said yourself she was a good worker. I'd have let her stay. *(Eric, Act One)*

Absent from Act Two entirely, Eric does the right thing by returning in Act Three to face the Inspector's interrogation. During the evening, both Eric and Gerald leave the Birling house to reflect upon what they have done. While Gerald is walking, he seeks to assure himself of the identity of the Inspector. However, Eric goes out **'to cool off'** *(Act Two)* and returns determined to accept his responsibility. Despite evidence of previous dishonesty, Priestley seems to be suggesting that Eric is the better man.

Tips for assessment

Make sure you have thought about the comparisons that can be made between different characters in the play. There are many interesting parallels and contrasts worth exploring.

Activity 12

1. Make three further comparisons of the way in which Priestley presents the relationship that Eric and Gerald have with Eva Smith. You could draw a table with two columns like the one below to record your ideas.

Eric Birling	Gerald Croft

2. Who do you think behaves in the worse way towards Eva? Write two paragraphs explaining your views with close reference to the text.

When Eric hears about his mother's refusal to assist Eva, he is devastated, **'you killed her – and the child she'd have had, too – my child – your own grandchild'** *(Act Three)*. Like Sheila, Eric seems unlikely to forget the lessons he has learned in his encounter with the Inspector. Eric is linked with the themes of responsibility, class, shame and blame, secrets and lies.

Gerald Croft

Priestley describes Gerald in the stage directions, as ***'an attractive chap about thirty, rather too manly to be a dandy but very much the easy well-bred young man-about-town'*** *(Act One)*. Aged 30, Gerald is one of the younger generation but he is more worldly-wise than Eric and Sheila, who are both described as being in their early twenties. His experience in his father's business leads him to support all of the decisions that Mr Birling made in relation to sacking Eva Smith, agreeing, **'we'd have done the same thing'** *(Act One)*.

As the play progresses we begin to see a less 'attractive' side to Gerald emerging and, ultimately, it appears that, like the Birlings, he is too much set in his ways to be seriously affected by the Inspector's revelations.

Gerald lied to Sheila about where he was the previous summer, assuring her in Act One that **'I was awfully busy at the works all that time'** *(Act One)*. In fact, he was keeping Daisy Renton as his mistress. In Act Two, by pretending that he is trying to protect Shelia, he attempts to prevent her from hearing the truth about his relationship. Priestley uses Sheila's sarcasm, in this Act, to help the audience to see the hypocrisy behind Gerald's apparently charitable actions towards Daisy.

Gerald claims that he responded to Daisy's **'cry for help'** *(Act Two)* in avoiding Alderman Meggarty's attentions and that he found her something to eat and somewhere to stay. He glosses over the fact that, although he says he **'didn't ask for anything in return'** *(Act Two)*, he eventually seduced Daisy and kept her in a suite of rooms that cost him nothing and made her leave before the owner, Charlie Brunswick, returned from Canada. He reveals that he gave her **'a parting gift of enough money – though it wasn't so very much – to see her through to the end of the year'** *(Act Two)* and that after that he **'never saw her again'** *(Act Two)*, having evidently never made enquiries about her.

Although he leaves the Birling house **'to be alone for a little while'** because he is **'rather more – upset – by this business than I probably appear to be'** *(Act Two)*, he never once accepts his responsibility in helping to ruin the girl and he returns bent on disproving the identity of the Inspector and making light of the damage done to Eva.

The Inspector questions Gerald Croft in the 2009 National Theatre production

Inspector Goole

Priestley is deliberately vague about the identity of the Inspector but one thing is clearly established – he is not an ordinary police officer.

When he arrives in Act One, Priestley's stage directions describe the Inspector as creating at once ***'an impression of massiveness, solidity and purposefulness'***. Like Birling, he is a man ***'in his fifties'*** and he has a particular way of speaking, ***'carefully, weightily'*** with a habit of ***'looking hard at the person he addresses before actually speaking'***.

Activity 16

Pick out what you consider to be the key words from Priestley's description of the Inspector in the stage directions above. How are these characteristics likely to influence the audience?

As the play progresses, the audience, like Sheila, begins to suspect the Inspector of having a superior knowledge of the private affairs of the Birling family and of Gerald Croft that goes far beyond what might have been gleaned from a **'rough sort of diary'** *(Act Two)* belonging to the dead girl.

Furthermore, unlike a police officer whose routine method of investigation would be to conduct his inquiries in private, Inspector Goole reveals the individual 'offences' of the characters communally so that there is always at least one other person present when 'confessions' are made.

Activity 17

Why do you think Priestley decided to have the Inspector question each 'suspect' in front of witnesses? How does this add to the dramatic impact of their 'confessions'? Give reasons for your views.

Key quotations

Public men, Mr Birling, have responsibilities as well as privileges.
(Inspector, Act Two)

She came to you for help [...] you not only refused it yourself but saw to it that others refused it too [...] you slammed the door in her face.
(Inspector, Act Two)

By Act Three, the Inspector is ready to conclude his investigations and to deliver his verdict on the death of Eva Smith. Having established, in a twist of the whodunit genre, that every suspect is guilty of having a part in Eva's death, the Inspector appears to hand out a 'sentence' to them all, which is that they should **'Never forget'** *(Act Three)*. He reviews each of the crimes committed against Eva and is particularly scathing to Mrs Birling and to Mr Birling – **'You started it'** *(Act Three)*.

The Inspector's final words of the play are the least likely to come from a 'real' police inspector as Goole warns the family about the potential consequences of their selfish actions.

Key quotations

And I tell you that the time will soon come when, if men will not learn that lesson, then they will be taught it in fire and blood and anguish. Good night. *(Inspector, Act Three)*

Inspector Goole in the 2009 National Theatre production

Activity 18

Discuss the following questions and be prepared to share your ideas with the class:

1. What effects do you think Priestley intended to create by making a mystery of the Inspector's identity?
2. Look through the play to find textual evidence to support your personal interpretation(s) of the Inspector's possible identity.

Minor characters

Edna

An Edwardian parlour maid whose duties would include opening the door to guests

Edna has a minor role, but she does perform a function in the play. She announces the arrival of the Inspector, which helps to establish his identity as a 'flesh and blood' character in the play rather than a ghostly apparition.

Edna also represents one of millions of ordinary people that the Inspector refers to at the end of the play, whose **'lives [...] hopes and fears'** *(Act Three)* are bound up with everyone else's. As a maid to the Birlings, she represents another poorly paid person who supports their comfortable lifestyle. You may notice that both Mr and Mrs Birling give Edna orders but never thank her for her services.

Characters that do not appear

Eva Smith

Although Eva Smith never appears on stage, the audience receives enough information to build up quite a clear picture of her:

- early twenties; very pretty with soft brown hair and big dark eyes
- a country girl whose parents are both dead
- a good worker with some spirit and resourcefulness
- a romantic girl who is gracious when 'dropped' by Gerald
- a principled girl; despite her lowly status and eventual decline into a form of prostitution, she will not accept stolen money or incriminate Eric any further.

Tips for assessment

Upgrade

Remember that although Eva is very significant within the plot of the play, she is not strictly a 'character' within it. So if you are asked in the exam 'Who do you consider to be the most sympathetic character in *An Inspector Calls*?' you should not choose Eva Smith.

While the audience is able to form an impression of Eva's appearance and character, we cannot discount the possibility that Gerald is correct and that she represents a series of different girls who have all been harmed by coming into contact with him and the Birlings. The name, Eva Smith – a combination of the name of the first woman, Eve, and the most common surname in Britain, Smith – signifies that Eva is an **everywoman** figure.

everywoman like 'everyman', a representative of all human beings

Activity 19

What effect does Priestley create for the audience by choosing to portray Eva as a representative 'everywoman' figure, rather than an individual character?

Writing about characters

Upgrade

In your exam you may be asked to write about one or more characters. When answering this type of question, it is important to focus on the methods Priestley uses to present each character and how he uses the character to communicate his ideas to an audience.

Try to consider the following methods of presentation, where relevant:

- what the character looks/sounds like
- what the character says about himself/herself and about others
- what others say about the character
- how the character might be compared/contrasted with other characters
- what the character does – his/her actions and/or reactions in the play
- what kind of language the character uses when speaking.

When thinking about the purpose or function of the character, you should consider the following possible uses:

- to give/receive information
- to develop the plot
- to comment on or to represent specific themes
- to act as a foil or contrast to other characters
- to alter the mood or atmosphere: for example, to add humour or pathos
- to act as a 'catalyst' (bringing about change in the story)
- to act as a mouthpiece for the playwright's views.

Stage directions

When we are reading a play, rather than watching one, we are aware of two different aspects of language in the text: the stage directions and the characters' dialogue.

The stage directions express the playwright's intentions for the way the play is presented. In Act One, for example, the directions tell us that the play is set in ***'The dining-room of a fairly large suburban house'*** and Priestley offers directions (in brackets) for the delivery of some of the lines, such as '[***angrily***]', '[***warningly***]', '[***relieved***]'.

Character speech

The second type of language is the dialogue between characters and it is through the way that the characters speak – as well as through what they say – that the playwright is able to shape and present character.

Mr Birling

Priestley tells us in the stage directions that Mr Birling is ***'rather provincial in his speech'*** *(Act One)* and this is revealed through what he chooses to talk about and through the words he uses to express himself. On stage the actor playing Birling might, for example, be the only actor to speak with a slight Midlands accent as Birling is a 'self-made' man.

Before the Inspector arrives, Mr Birling's speeches are dominated by his sense of self-importance. In particular, he assumes the voice of experience to offer advice about the future. His tone is emphatic and his manner is blunt, often blustering; he tends to speak in quite short, uncomplicated sentences and uses straightforward vocabulary. He uses the personal pronouns – 'I', 'me' and 'we' – very frequently.

Birling betrays a lack of 'good breeding' by discussing money and profit on the occasion of his daughter's engagement (and at the dinner table). In fact, throughout the play, Mr Birling refers frequently to money, costs and prices; this shows the audience where his priorities lie.

Key quotations

They worked us hard in those days and kept us short of cash.
(Mr Birling, Act One)

Fifty pounds – on top of drinking and going round the town! Where did you get fifty pounds from?
(Mr Birling, Act Three)

Money

In 1912, £50 would have been equivalent to over £4,000 in today's money.

Activity 1

Look closely at Mr Birling's speech, in Act One, about what a good time it is for Gerald and Sheila to marry:

Key quotations

... I say, you can ignore all this silly pessimistic talk. When you marry, you'll be marrying at a very good time. Yes, a very good time – and soon it'll be an even better time. Last month, just because the miners came out on strike, there's a lot of wild talk about possible labour trouble in the near future. Don't worry. We've passed the worst of it. We employers at last are coming together to see that our interests – and the interests of Capital – are properly protected. And we're in for a time of steadily increasing prosperity.

How does Priestley use words and sentence structure in this extract to convey Birling's character? Write a paragraph explaining your ideas and use quotations to support your points.

Another feature of Mr Birling's speech which emerges when he is angry or frustrated is his tendency to use terse phrases of exasperation, bordering on swearing and inappropriate for a gentleman of the time.

Key quotations

[*angrily*]: **Why the devil do you want to go upsetting the child like that?** *(Mr Birling, Act One)*

Damned impudence! *(Mr Birling, Act Two)*

Look – for God's sake! *(Mr Birling, Act Three)*

Activity 2

Given Mr Birling's 'explosive' nature and his tendency to protest when he doesn't like what he is hearing, imagine what the interview with Eva Smith must have been like when she was asking for higher wages.

In pairs, create a short scene between Mr Birling and Eva where she asked for fairer pay.

Mrs Birling

Mrs Birling has a higher social status than her husband so the actress playing this role would be more likely to speak with a more refined accent than he does. In Act One Mrs Birling says very little but when she does speak, especially in Act Two, she uses a generally dismissive tone. She has a patronizing attitude towards her children and clearly sees the Inspector as an inferior being. This is reflected in the language she uses, which is often negative.

Mrs Birling is very haughty and treats the Inspector as an inferior

Key quotations

I don't know what you're talking about, Sheila. *(Mrs Birling, Act Two)*

Please don't contradict me like that. *(Mrs Birling to Sheila, Act Two)*

[*sharply*]: Sheila, don't talk nonsense. *(Mrs Birling, Act Two)*

I don't think we need discuss it. *(Mrs Birling, Act Two)*

Activity 3

1. Go through Mrs Birling's speeches in Act Two and make a list of every instance where she uses a negative: for example, 'don't', 'not', 'nothing', 'didn't', 'wasn't', 'shouldn't'.
2. What impression does this give you about her character? Write a paragraph explaining your views.

Sheila and Eric Birling

Sheila and Eric represent the younger generation and one of the ways that Priestley conveys their youth is through their use of 'modern' **slang** (for 1912) and **colloquialisms**. For example, Sheila accuses Eric of being **'squiffy'** *(Act One)* at the beginning of the play, causing Mrs Birling to complain about **'the things you girls pick up these days!'** *(Act One)*. Sheila also calls Eric an **'ass'** and, later in the Act, a **'chump'** *(Act One)*.

Eric uses the same kind of slang as Sheila and speaks in a casual manner; for example, when he discusses women's attitudes towards clothes, he says, **'Women are potty about 'em'** *(Act One)*. When commenting on his father's 'good advice', he says **'you've piled it on a bit tonight, Father'** *(Act One)*. Eric's crudest form of colloquial speech occurs in Act Three where he refers to the prostitutes that he has seen with his father's friends as **'fat old tarts round the town'** *(Act Three)*.

Activity 4

1. Find out who uses the following slang expressions in Act One and suggest modern equivalents for each phrase:
   a) **I call it tough luck.** *(Act One)*
   b) **Well, I think it's a dam' shame.** *(Act One)*
   c) **It's a rotten shame.** *(Act One)*
   d) **I think it was a mean thing to do.** *(Act One)*
   e) **I think I'd better turn in.** *(Act One)*
2. As well as highlighting Sheila and Eric's youth, what else might their use of slang expressions reveal about them?

Sheila's language has an additional dimension to Eric's, in that she frequently interjects and interrupts the dialogue between other characters, rather than merely responding to questions. As the play progresses, she appears almost to become an 'accomplice' to the Inspector in his quest for the truth. Sometimes she is **sarcastic** in tone, especially during the Inspector's questioning of Gerald. At other times she tries to prevent her family from attempting to mislead the Inspector.

Key quotations

[*with sharp sarcasm*]: **Of course not. You were the wonderful Fairy Prince.** *(Sheila, Act Two)*

[*urgently, cutting in*]: **Mother, don't – please don't. For your own sake, as well as ours, you mustn't –** *(Sheila to Mrs Birling, Act Two)*

colloquial speech informal, everyday speech

sarcasm a tone of voice often used in a mocking way, suggesting that the speaker is not sincere in what he or she is saying

slang distinctive phrases and vocabulary shared by a particular group of people

Activity 5

Look again at the last page of dialogue in Act Two which begins with Mrs Birling's line, **'And he ought to be dealt with very severely'** and ends with the fall of the curtain.

1. Sheila has four fairly brief lines here; what is the effect of Sheila's repeated interruptions?
2. How might an actress perform these lines to reveal her motives at this point in the play?

Gerald Croft

While Gerald does use some slang, marking him out as one of the younger characters, his responses to the unfolding events are more mature and more measured than those of the Birling siblings. Despite his show of emotion when he realizes that 'Daisy' has died a horrible death, he is still able to think clearly and his speech is a product of that rational thought process. The actor playing Gerald would be likely to be well spoken with no trace of a Midlands accent.

Key quotations

A man comes here pretending to be a police officer. It's a hoax of some kind. Now what does he do? Very artfully, working on bits of information he's picked up here and there, he bluffs us into confessing that we've all been mixed up in this girl's life in one way or another. *(Gerald, Act Three)*

Activity 6

1. Read the key quotation above and identify:

   a) words and phrases that suggest Gerald is youthful

   b) features of his speech that suggest Gerald is clear-headed and a rational thinker.
2. What impact do the characteristics above have on you as an audience?
3. What does his speech suggest about his position in society?

Tips for assessment

When writing about Priestley's language, make sure that you include reference to his stage directions as well as to the individual speeches of the characters.

The Inspector

The Inspector's character is one of great power and impressiveness, yet Priestley is clear in his stage directions that the actor ***'need not be a big man'*** *(Act One)*. His power, therefore, must come from what he says and the deliberate manner in which he says it: ***'He speaks carefully, weightily'*** *(Act One)*. The Inspector claims that he is **'Only recently transferred'** *(Act One)* to Brumley so it is unlikely that the actor would have a Midlands accent, nor would a police inspector at this time speak with **Received Pronunciation**; a clear and fairly neutral voice would be appropriate for the actor playing this role.

The Inspector's use of language is quite unlike that of the rest of the cast. He speaks, for the most part, emphatically, steadily and without hesitation. Although he asks many questions over the course of the play, it is his observations about what each character did to Eva and his pronouncements about responsibility that present him at his most powerful.

The way in which the Inspector speaks is forceful and demands attention

Activity 7

Find at least three examples from the text where the Inspector offers his judgement on the way one of the characters acted or behaved. For each example, comment on how Priestley uses language to lend weight or emphasis to the Inspector's words.

Received Pronunciation the term used for a standard English accent, with no trace of a regional influence; it is sometimes called 'the Queen's English'.

The Inspector sometimes uses a series of three brief phrases or simple sentences, in order to leave a lasting impression on the Birlings. This literary device is sometimes known as a **triple**. Here are some examples:

Key quotations

It's the way I like to go to work. One person and one line of inquiry at a time. Otherwise, there's a muddle. *(Inspector, Act One)*

[*harshly*]: **Yes, but you can't. It's too late. She's dead.** *(Inspector, Act One)*

We don't live alone. We are members of one body. We are responsible for each other. *(Inspector, Act Three)*

triple A 'triple' is a literary device that uses the combination of three short statements, adjectives or adverbs to add emphasis to an idea or argument.

The Inspector also uses language more imaginatively than the other older characters and sometimes creates an effective rhythm or echo within individual speeches that add to their impact, for example:

Key quotations

Because what happened to her then may have determined what happened to her afterwards, and what happened to her afterwards may have driven her to suicide. *(Inspector, Act One)*

Because she'd been turned out and turned down too many times. *(Inspector, Act Two)*

You made her pay a heavy price for that. And now she'll make you pay a heavier price still. *(Inspector, Act Three)*

Activity 8

Re-read the Inspector's final speech, which he delivers just before he leaves the Birlings to their consciences. Discuss the following questions and make notes:

1. How many different linguistic techniques can you identify within the speech?
2. What does the use of language suggest to you about the Inspector's ideas, attitudes and values?
3. Write your ideas up into two paragraphs explaining how Priestley uses language to create a strong impression of the Inspector's character.

Figurative language

Priestley uses very little **figurative language** in the play and, where he does, it tends to be in the form of common **clichés** and everyday sayings. This helps to keep the language realistic and, as we have seen, the speech varies, as in real life, from character to character.

Key quotations

A chain of events. *(Inspector, Act One)*

... as if we were all mixed up together like bees in a hive *(Mr Birling, Act One)*

I don't propose to give you much more rope. *(Mr Birling, Act Two)*

You mustn't try to build up a kind of wall between us and that girl. If you do, then the Inspector will just break it down. *(Sheila, Act Two)*

cliché a 'well-worn' expression or saying that is lacking in originality

figurative language the term for any kind of phrase or sentence that is not literal; figurative language includes metaphors and similes

Activity 9

Create a spider diagram to record some of your ideas about the use of 'everyday' language in the play. Write the words 'Language use' in the centre of your spider diagram. Add notes to the diagram in response to the following questions:

1. What might the lack of figurative language suggest about the characters?
2. Why do you think Priestley decided to base the dialogue on 'everyday' language rather than including lots of complicated figurative language?

Writing about language

Upgrade

Whatever question you answer as part of your assessment, you should think about and comment on Priestley's use of language. This includes his choice of vocabulary, his use of sentence structure and the organization and sequence of the dialogue between characters. For example, you could think about:

- the way Priestley uses language to differentiate between the generations as well as to create distinctive voices
- the way Priestley creates a sense of tone through each character's use of vocabulary and the structure of their dialogue
- the power of the Inspector's speech patterns in particular.

Time and timing

The Inspector implies that time is running out, on many different levels

An Inspector Calls can be described as one of Priestley's 'time' plays because it explores the relationship between the past, present and future; some people who have watched and studied the play have even suggested that the Inspector is some sort of 'cosmic time-lord'.

The revelation at the end of Act Three that a girl has just died and that an inspector is on his way suggests that 'real' time has in some way been distorted or manipulated by the Inspector, who appears to carry out his investigation under the increasing pressure of time, **'my trouble is – that I haven't much time** *(Act Three)*. Indeed, throughout the play, there are over a hundred direct references to time or timing.

It is no coincidence that, before the Inspector arrives to investigate events that have happened in the past, Mr Birling speaks with (misplaced) confidence about the future. Towards the end of the play, the Inspector prophesies the very real **'fire and blood and anguish'** *(Act Three)* that will be the two world wars. Then, just as Mr and Mrs Birling and Gerald are putting the events of the night behind them, the telephone call announces that their ordeal is about to begin all over again.

Activity 1

Use the Internet to research the 'time theories' of P.D. Ouspensky and J.W. Dunne, whose books, *A New Model of the Universe* (1931) and *An Experiment with Time* (1927), stimulated Priestley to write about time in his plays. Create a fact sheet, summarizing some of the key ideas connected with these theories.

Activity 2

Plan an answer to the following essay question:

How does Priestley use 'time' to make the play more exciting and dramatic?

Select examples from the text to support your ideas.

A notable characteristic of the Inspector's inquiries is his ability to pinpoint precisely when each event leading to Eva's suicide took place. Referring to **'a letter'** and **'a sort of diary'** *(Act One)* that Eva left at her lodgings, the Inspector creates a complete timeline of Eva's life from her dismissal from Birling's factory up to her death.

Activity 3

The Inspector is able to map out each character's past actions in detail. How does this mysterious ability add to the dramatic impact of the play? Write three or four paragraphs in answer to this question. In your answer, think about:

- how the Inspector's attitude contrasts with the way the other characters regard their past actions
- the idea of responsibility
- Priestley's overall message in the play.

Responsibility

Undoubtedly, the most important message of the play relates to personal responsibility and public duty.

The Inspector, speaking for Priestley, wants to demonstrate how every action and interaction can have an impact on others. Through the device of Eva Smith – one girl who was dealt with thoughtlessly by each of the Birlings and Gerald Croft – he shows how a series of wrongs ultimately brings about tragic consequences: **'You'll be able to divide the responsibility between you when I've gone'** *(Act Three)*.

Eva Smith is not the only victim of these interactions since, as a result of their thoughtless actions, Mr Birling will forfeit his knighthood, Mrs Birling will lose her position as the head of a women's charity, Eric may well be charged with fraud and Gerald may have lost Sheila for good; Sheila will never recover from her sense of guilt.

Tips for assessment

Assessment questions frequently focus on prominent themes from the play; however, sometimes the themes may be expressed differently from what you might be expecting. For example, 'Class, money, power and privilege' could be referred to as 'status and wealth'. When thinking about themes, therefore, it's always useful to think about alternative descriptions for them.

Activity 4

Explore the methods Priestley uses to emphasize the theme of responsibility in the play.

1. Create a larger copy of the table below.
2. For each method listed in the table, explain how Priestley uses it to convey ideas about responsibility and the effects it creates.
3. Add references and quotations that will be useful for your revision.

Theme: Responsibility		
Dramatic method	**How does Priestley use this method to present the theme?**	**Example quotations**
The plot	Think about: • the focus of the inquiry upon responsibility • the significance of the beginning and the ending.	
Characters	Think about: • Mr Birling's responsibilities as an employer, magistrate and father • Mrs Birling's responsibilities as Chairwoman of a charity and as a mother • the responsibilities brought by wealth and position • the Inspector's responsibility to discover the truth.	
Dialogue	Think about: • individual characters' direct comments about responsibility	
Vocabulary	Think about: • figurative language related to responsibility • repetition • irony.	
Related themes	Think about: • how references to duty, power and influence support the theme of responsibility.	

In 1912, many wealthy families took their servants for granted

The theme of responsibility is bound up with other repeated ideas in the play, including:

- class, money, power and privilege
- guilt and blame
- selfishness.

Activity 5

Select one of the themes above and create a set of notes on the methods Priestley uses to explore the theme in the play.

Use the table on page 64 as a template. You should replace the bullet points with your own ideas.

Secrecy and lies

The Inspector has the task of uncovering the truth and cutting through the lies that the characters tell themselves, and each other, as well as those that they try to tell him.

Mr Birling has no secrets. He sacked a girl for causing trouble and is quite open in admitting it: **'I was quite justified'** *(Act One)*. As the play proceeds and he begins to see the possibility of his knighthood disappearing under the pressure of a scandal, he becomes alarmed. When Eric's theft is revealed, his first instinct is not an honest one: **'I've got to cover this up as soon as I can'** *(Act Three)*.

Activity 6

1. Look at the following list of untruths. Which character does each one relate to?
   a) Concealed having kept a mistress the previous summer
   b) Concealed an alcohol problem
   c) Lied to the manager of Milwards about Eva's 'impertinence'
   d) Lied to Sheila about being busy at work
   e) Concealed the fact that he fathered a child.
2. Which character, in your opinion, is the most dishonest in the play? Write three paragraphs in answer to this question and give evidence to support your views.

Mrs Birling is the only character who lies directly to the Inspector when she claims she doesn't recognize the girl in the photograph. The Inspector's immediate response, **'You're not telling me the truth'** *(Act Two)*, brings an outraged reaction from both Mr and Mrs Birling until Mrs Birling is made to admit that she did see the girl and she did refuse her request for help.

Activity 7

Look again at the section in Act Two, from when the Inspector shows Mrs Birling the picture of Eva Smith to the moment when he tells Mrs Birling, **'You have no hope of not discussing it, Mrs Birling'**.

1. Look carefully at the language that Mrs Birling uses as she tries to avoid answering the Inspector's questions and make a list of her strategies in each case.
2. How might an actress perform each of her bluffs to show the audience that she is being dishonest? Think about:
   - hesitation/use of pause
   - eye-contact
   - tone of voice
   - use of emphasis
   - use of props.

Mrs Birling is shown to be a hypocrite when it appears that one of the things that prejudiced her against the girl was that she felt she was telling **'a pack of lies'** *(Act Two)*. She refuses to believe that the girl was trying to protect the father of her child and uses this to excuse her behaviour. Like Mr Birling, Mrs Birling believes she was **'perfectly justified'** *(Act Two)* in the heartless way she treated Eva.

Priestley uses the hypocrisy of the Birlings to criticize the class system which punishes the poor for the slightest evidence of dishonesty while the rich are able to 'cover up' and hide their lies behind a mask of respectability.

Other themes

An Inspector Calls could be described as a play of **contrasts**. Here is a list of other pairs of themes or motifs that appear in the play:

- rich and poor
- employers and workers
- innocence and guilt
- blame and shame
- appearance and reality
- love and lust.

contrast ideas and themes that are different from one another or represent opposite perspectives

Activity 8

Choose two or three themes that you have discovered in your study of the play and create a spider diagram for each theme. Include comments and examples showing how Priestley presents each theme and the effects this has on the audience.

Contrasts between Sheila/Eva show how life is different for the rich and poor.

Rich and poor

Priestley reveals how the rich make the poor poorer: 'it's my duty to keep labour costs down' (Birling, Act One).

Writing about themes

Upgrade

In your assessment you may be asked to write about an individual theme or pair of themes. There are different ways that questions about themes might be asked. Here are some examples.

1. You might be asked how Priestley presents a theme. For example:

   How does Priestley present the themes of power and privilege in *An Inspector Calls*?

   This type of question requires you to think about the methods that the playwright has used to convey this theme.

2. You might be asked a question that prompts you to consider the significance of the theme, for example:

   How important do you think the themes of guilt and remorse are in the play?

   To answer this type of question, you should think about how the theme relates to Priestley's main purpose and message and how it compares to other significant themes.

Writing for the stage is a special art. A playwright, like a novelist, has a story to tell and a purpose in telling it. However, a play is only complete when it is performed in front of an audience in production and this is the result of a collaboration between a director and a cast of actors, supported by a design team, responsible for setting and **props**, costume, lighting and sound design. This production team all work together on the playwright's **script** to find ways to bring the play to life in the theatre.

props the moveable objects used on stage by the actors

script a play becomes a script when it is being used by the production team in rehearsal for a performance

Interpretations of drama

As we read a play, we each become interpreters of the playwright's ideas. By reading both the stage directions and the dialogue, the reader will begin to see the play coming to life by visualizing the setting for each scene and imagining the characters' facial expressions and movements as they speak the lines. This is a form of 'interpretation'.

By reading carefully, the reader may begin to notice recurrent ideas, repeated words or issues that the characters appear to be most concerned about. In *An Inspector Calls*, for example, the Birlings seem highly sensitive to social position, while the Inspector is more concerned about social responsibility.

This careful approach to reading the text is also the first step that a director has to take before staging the play, where he or she will work with set, costume and technical designers to present their interpretation to an audience, who must also actively 'interpret' what they see on stage.

Activity 1

Which of the following statements represent interpretations of *An Inspector Calls* and which statements are based simply on what is written?

a) Daisy and Eva are the same person.

b) The Inspector arrives at the Birling household in order to interview the Birlings and Gerald Croft.

c) Mrs Birling refuses to help Eva when she asks for help.

d) The Inspector is a cosmic time-lord.

e) Eric is jealous of his father's respect for Gerald.

f) At the end of the play Gerald decides that the Inspector was a hoaxer.

The play in production

The director

Sometimes, if a play has been written recently, the playwright may be involved in the production process. However, often the playwright's involvement ends when the writing is complete. From this point forwards, the director has free rein in interpreting the play for the audience.

Most directors try to respect the intentions of the playwright and, where there are stage directions, setting requirements or notes on characters included by the writer, they will follow them. Some directors take a fresh approach to each play they tackle and, in production, may give emphasis to some themes rather than others or may present a particular character in a new way.

For example, Priestley deliberately presents the Inspector as an **ambiguous** character. Is he a ghost? Is he a crank? Is he a time-traveller? A director needs to make his or her mind up about this before directing the play, even if he or she wants to retain some level of ambiguity for the audience. This is because the mystery surrounding the 'true' identity of the Inspector will have an impact on how the whole play will be perceived by the audience.

ambiguous where the meaning is not clear or where something has at least two possible meanings

In the 2009 National Theatre production, the Inspector and other cast members appeared in costumes from the 1940s in contrast to those worn by the Birlings

Activity 2

1. Choose two possible identities that might fit the Inspector, supporting your ideas with specific references to the text.
2. Make suggestions about how you might direct the actor in each 'version' of the role to convey your interpretation of the Inspector's identity to the audience.

A director must also work with the actors to determine how sympathetically or unsympathetically individual characters are to be presented on stage. For example, it is possible for the actor playing Gerald to appear to be genuinely remorseful about his relationship with Daisy and to suffer real distress as he tells his story to the Inspector.

On the other hand, he could appear deliberately evasive, both with Sheila and the Inspector, and somewhat self-satisfied in having done Daisy a good turn – rescuing her from 'old Meggarty', feeding her, housing her and giving her an allowance. His assumption that Sheila will accept the ring again, after all his secrets have been disclosed, could suggest a lack of sensitivity.

Activity 3

Working together in small groups, each with one 'director', try acting out brief sections of the text that involve Gerald and see how many different interpretations of the role you can achieve.

Much like a student of the play, a director will read and re-read the play many times before making crucial decisions about what he or she wants the audience to take away from the performance.

The director probes the text, thinking about the effects he or she wishes to achieve for the audience. For example, should the audience be made to confront the evils of capitalism? Or is it more important for them to re-think their attitudes to their own actions? Making decisions like these will help the director to create his or her individual interpretation of the play.

Other decisions that have to be made by a director relate to the acting and to the design of the play.

The actors

Priestley offers brief descriptions of each character in his stage directions. For example, we are told that Mrs Birling is *'a rather cold woman'* *(Act One)* and Sheila is *'a pretty girl in her early twenties'* *(Act One)*. This gives the director a fairly free hand when choosing actors for the roles. Similarly Priestley has offered some indication of the way that Mr Birling speaks – *'rather provincial in his speech'* *(Act One)* – but does not specify anything about the type of voices that the others have.

Casting

When casting actors to perform the play, the director will be looking for particular physical qualities, in terms of age, build, facial features and vocal qualities that best fit each character. Actors are often able to perform in any accent but tend to be restricted in terms of whether they have a high-pitched or a deep voice.

Activity 4

Imagine you are putting on a performance of *An Inspector Calls*. Write down the physical and vocal qualities that you would want each actor to possess. For each character, decide:

a) What his or her build and height should be, together with any further physical characteristics that you think are important (e.g. you might want Gerald to have a square jawline to emphasize his masculinity).

b) What his or her voice should be like (e.g. try to suggest a pitch, pace and accent for each character).

c) Give reasons for your choices based on your knowledge of the text.

All the characters show a range of different emotions at different points in the play, so the director and actors must work together to achieve what should appear to the audience as a set of three-dimensional and believable characters.

We have seen that Priestley occasionally uses stage directions to tell the actors how to deliver their lines; but there are many occasions when he does not offer any guidance. This is where the input of a good director is needed to allow the actors to present the characters in a way that is consistent with the director's overall interpretation of the play.

Activity 5

Look again at the section of text in Act Two from the end of Gerald's 'interrogation', when the Inspector says: **'It's all I want to know from you'** to Gerald's exit, after Gerald says: **'I don't think so. Excuse me'**.

1. Imagine you have to direct this section on stage. Add a brief stage direction to go in brackets before each of the speeches in this section to guide the actor in how to deliver the lines.
2. Write a paragraph explaining the stage directions you have added and how these support your interpretation of the characters at this point in the play. Include your thoughts on Sheila, Gerald, Mr and Mrs Birling and the Inspector.

Body language

When the play is performed on stage, it communicates its messages and themes to the audience through more than just the spoken word. In addition to listening to the dialogue, a theatre audience makes sense of the play by watching the actors bring the characters to life: by seeing how they act when they are speaking and how they react, physically and facially, to the unfolding events.

Body language and facial expressions were used to dramatic effect in the 2009 National Theatre production

The director needs to help the actors to use non-verbal communication to reinforce their presentation of the characters even when they are not speaking. Some examples of non-verbal stage communication are included in the table below:

Type of non-verbal communication	Examples
1. Body language	Standing up or turning sharply to protest; sitting down to show defeat; turning away to show guilt or shame
2. Use of pause	Blank stare or look of shock
3. Eye contact/ eye-line	Shifting eye-line from a character's face to the floor to show guilt; glaring/staring to convey meaning
4. Physical contact	Touching to comfort or restrain; kissing to show affection
5. Use of space	Moving towards another character to show intimacy, to congratulate them or to comfort them; approaching a character to threaten them; moving away from a character to evade them
6. Tears	Crying/sobbing to show sadness or shock
7. Facial expressions	Smiling, frowning, looks of confusion, contentment, neutrality
8. Interactions with objects	Fidgeting with clothes, tapping fingers, shuffling to show discomfort, agitation, embarrassment or apprehension

Activity 6

Use the grid above to help you build up a picture of how each character might behave and react on stage. For each character, provide examples from the text where specific forms of non-verbal communication would be appropriate. Include quotations of relevant lines from the play where you can.

Activity 7

Look at the sections of interaction between Sheila and Gerald at the end of Act One and the beginning of Act Two from **'SHEILA: ...Well Gerald?'** to **'SHEILA: Yes, but you don't believe me. And this is just the wrong time not to believe me'**.

How does Sheila's use of 'non-verbal' methods of communication help you to understand her character here?

Stage setting

A stage designer will work closely with the director to achieve the setting that the director wants. In the stage directions at the very beginning of *An Inspector Calls*, Priestley offers quite a detailed description of the dining room that is to be the setting for the entire play.

Key quotations

The dining-room of a fairly large suburban house, belonging to a prosperous manufacturer. It has good solid furniture of the period. The general effect is substantial and heavily comfortable, but not cosy and homelike. *(Act One)*

Priestley's stage directions suggest that the director/designer should try to create a formal space rather than a 'cosy' one. However, Priestley is not overly prescriptive in his staging requirements, suggesting that if they so wish, **'Producers'** (another term for directors) may **'dispense with an ordinary realistic set'** *(Act One)*.

If a director decides to dispense with **theatrical realism** in the setting, other possible theatrical styles include **selective realism** and **expressionism**. Certain plays will be better suited to particular styles.

expressionism an expressionistic setting is likely to be abstract; for example, the set may represent certain themes of the play or attempt to portray the inner feelings of individual characters, creating a dream-like or nightmarish vision of reality

selective realism a setting where only the props and furniture that are needed, used or referred to in the play appear on stage and there is no attempt to create the impression of completely realistic surroundings

theatrical realism where the setting attempts to represent real life on stage, with detailed sets and convincing surroundings

Activity 8

Which style, in your opinion, would best suit a production of *An Inspector Calls*? Justify your views with reference to the text.

Whatever style the director chooses for the production, it's important that the wealth of the Birlings is conveyed to the audience and that they see, through the theatrical 'signs' used – such as set, costume and props – that the family are used to a life of luxury.

Solid, expensive-looking furniture, richly coloured fabrics and sparkling glass and silverware would help to convey the comfort of the Birlings, which is harshly contrasted by the mental picture that the Inspector creates of a girl **'with no work, no money coming in, and living in lodgings, with no relatives to help her, few friends, lonely, half-starved...'** *(Act One)*.

Activity 9

Try designing a stage setting for the play; ask yourself how your ideas will help to convey Priestley's themes and intentions to the audience.

Costume

While a director may dispense with realism in terms of setting, few would choose any other style of costume than realistic. In order to exploit Priestley's 1912 period setting to the full, directors and designers tend to work together to create meticulously authentic Edwardian costumes, with exquisite evening gowns for Mrs Birling and Sheila and evening dress – white tie and tails – for the men at the party.

A glamorous evening gown designed in 1912

White tie and tails

A traditional form of formal evening wear for gentlemen – still worn, today, for events such as ceremonial dinners or grand balls. The outfit consists of a black jacket, known as an evening 'tailcoat', worn over a white shirt, with a white waistcoat and white bow-tie. The trousers are black to match the jacket.

The more elaborate and ornamented the dresses of the ladies, the more jewels worn and the more elegant their accessories, the more vicious it will appear of Mr Birling to have denied his workers an extra two shillings and sixpence per week because **'we'd have added about twelve per cent to our labour costs'** *(Act One)*.

Activity 10

Imagine that you are the costume designer for a production of *An Inspector Calls*; how might you use costume to emphasize the traits of particular characters? For example, you might like to think about Mrs Birling's cold personality, Sheila's vanity and the ambiguity of the Inspector's identity.

You may like to sketch your ideas, to support your description of the costumes. You will need to consider the period setting of the play as well as:

- colour
- fabric
- cut and fit
- accessories (gloves, hats/head-gear, jewellery, fans, watches, shoes).

Props

Most of the props used in this play serve the same purpose as the set and costumes: to highlight the wealth and status of the family. When the curtain opens, Edna is clearing ***'champagne glasses, etc., and then replacing them with decanter of port, cigar box and cigarettes. Port glasses are already on the table'*** *(Act One)*.

Not only are the Birlings able to enjoy a good meal; it is served on fine tableware and glassware. Priestley uses these physical objects on stage to contrast with the life of Eva, as well as the lives of a whole class of **'young women counting their pennies in their dingy little back bedrooms'** *(Act One)*.

Activity 11

1. Find at least three examples from the play where Priestley refers to Eva's living conditions.
2. For each example, explain how Priestley uses language to highlight the difference between the wealth of the Birlings that we see on stage and Eva's poverty that we are made to imagine, 'off-stage'.

Other key props include the photograph of the girl that the Inspector shows to Birling, Sheila and Mrs Birling, and the engagement ring. Both of these are significant.

One of the things that a director will have thought about in interpreting the play is whether or not the girl who each of the Birlings and Gerald came into contact with was **'the same girl'** *(Act Three)*. Gerald argues that **'There were probably four or five different girls'** *(Act Three)*, while Sheila and Eric insist that it doesn't matter if there was one or more than one, **'Everything we said had happened really had happened'** *(Act Three)*. In performance, the way that the actor handles the photograph, where he keeps it, how he reveals it and how he then conceals it from the others, will affect whether or not the audience is able to believe that **'He could have used a different photograph each time'** *(Act Three)*.

The Inspector only shows the photograph to one person at a time

The engagement ring is symbolic of love and trust. Gerald first offers it to Sheila in Act One, **'just at the right moment'**. Sheila accepts it despite clearly having some suspicion about where Gerald was the previous summer when **'you never came near me'** *(Act One)*. She is delighted with the ring, which must have cost a great deal of money, and she promises, **'I'll never let it go out of my sight for an instant'** *(Act One)*.

Activity 12

1. Imagine you are directing the actors playing Gerald and Sheila in Acts One and Three where the ring is used. Make suggestions for the way each actor will handle the prop to show how the characters feel on each occasion.
2. Select a short extract from the play that involves the prop and act it out, in groups, to test out your ideas.

Tips for assessment

If you get the chance to see this play on stage, look out for the ways the actors use their props; discuss this aspect of the performance as a group afterwards and record your thoughts.

Lighting and sound design

Priestley makes few specific requirements for the lighting and sound design in the play but there is one significant lighting effect, which he insists upon for Act One, where he says in the stage directions: ***'The lighting should be pink and intimate until the INSPECTOR arrives, and then it should be brighter and harder'***.

This lighting cue occurs when Birling says, **'All right, Edna. Show him in here. Give us some more light'**. The stage direction indicates, **'Edna** ***does'*** *(Act One)*. In 1912, domestic houses would have had gaslights, which were controllable, and Edna would have turned up the light to coincide with an increase in white stage lights. The intention is perhaps to suggest that until the arrival of the Inspector, the Birlings and Gerald were not facing reality – possibly viewing their life, as they say, 'through rose-tinted spectacles'. The bright light of truth is then shone onto their previous actions.

Activity 13

Discuss the following questions:

1. Why do you think Priestley decided to suggest a link between light and truth?
2. How else could the use of lighting add to the drama of the play? You might consider:
    - the progress of the Inspector's line of inquiry
    - the use of Eva's photograph
    - how lighting might be used to add to characterization.

There are two sound effects of a doorbell; one signals the arrival of the Inspector in Act One and the other marks the return of Gerald Croft in Act Three. In Act Two we hear the sound of Eric shutting the front door as he leaves the house. At the end of the play the telephone rings to herald in the climactic news that an Inspector is **'on his way here – to ask some – questions –'** *(Act Three)*. Apart from these specified sound effects, the sounds of the play consist only of the different sounds of the actors' voices.

Activity 14

Why, in your opinion, did Priestley decide to limit the use of sound effects in the play to a few very distinct instances? How does this contribute to the mood and atmosphere of the play? Give reasons to support your views.

Film versions of the play

There are two accessible film versions of the play. One was produced for the BBC in 1982; it stars Bernard Hepton as the Inspector. Although some lines have been cut, it is a version that closely follows the original.

The 1954 film, starring Alastair Sim as the Inspector, is very entertaining but needs to be viewed with caution. In this version, we actually see Eva Smith, and all her dealings with the Birlings and Gerald are shown within the film. This means that some of the characters' lines from the play are spoken by the actress who plays Eva and we are able to see her working and living conditions, the Birling factory and the department store, Milwards. Because of this, the audience is in no doubt that Eva Smith and Daisy Renton are the **'same girl'** *(Act Three)*. This removes one of the unanswered questions from the play and is therefore an alteration of Priestley's original text.

The Inspector in his rocking chair before he mysteriously disappears, in the 1954 film

The director of the 1954 film made other changes, too. The Inspector's name is changed to 'Poole', removing the original possible link with 'ghoul'; however, the Inspector is depicted very clearly as a supernatural visitor. Inspector Poole appears in the dining room as if he has simply materialized (no announcement by Edna) and, at the end of the play, Mr Birling asks him to wait in his study while the family listens to Gerald's theory about the hoax. We see the Inspector making himself comfortable in a rocking chair but when Birling opens the study door to confront the 'imposter', we see only an empty rocking chair – still rocking, as ghostly music plays.

Differences between theatre and film

There are a number of crucial differences between film and theatre in terms of what a theatre director and a film director can potentially achieve.

	Plays performed on stage	Film versions of plays
Setting	The action of the play must be depicted in a single stage space; although the space may be 'transformed' into different settings, using techniques such as lighting and props to create the illusion of different locations.	The action may be depicted as occurring in different locations – both inside and outside – and in any part of the world. These settings will appear to be real.
The text	Most plays are produced in their entirety with few 'cuts' made to the text.	Directors often omit sections of text, preferring to replace them with film images of what is being said or described.
Action	References to events that occur 'off-stage' are used to give the audience necessary information to help them to understand the story.	'Off-stage' action may be portrayed in the film, becoming a fully realized part of the story.
Characters	Characters that do not appear on stage are referred to or described by the 'on-stage' actors.	The director may choose to use actors to portray these characters in the film, allowing the director to dispense with descriptions of them.
Audience	The audience choose who/what to watch on stage from their seat in the auditorium where they can see the whole stage.	The film director chooses every shot of the film; the audience must watch the character selected by the director – the audience experience is therefore more closely shaped by the director.
Performance	As the actors and action is 'live', no two performances (even when performed by the same cast) are ever identical.	The film performance is captured forever; it never changes.

Activity 15

1. Why do you think the director of the 1954 film, Guy Hamilton, decided to make the changes he did to Priestley's play?
2. How do you think these decisions are likely to affect the audience's experience of the drama?

Stage history

Writing so shortly after the end of the Second World War, Priestley could not find a suitable London theatre that was able to put the play into production immediately and so the play had its **debut** in Moscow before opening at the New Theatre in London in 1946 with Ralph Richardson in the role of the Inspector.

Early performances

The play initially received mixed reviews from the **critics**. J.C. Trewin, writing in *The Observer* newspaper, found the play too long; he complained that it **'could have been stripped to half its length'**, while the *Daily Mail* theatre critic Lionel Hale was disappointed in the ending, which he found offered **'a fatal dead-end'** rather than providing a **'theatrical solution'**. However, the play was well received by others, notably *The New Statesman*'s Stephen Potter, who admired the play for its **'beautiful craftsmanship'** and commented that the play's ending was the **'best coup de théâtre'** of the year.

Activity 16

Select one of the critics' comments mentioned above and write two paragraphs explaining whether you agree or disagree with the point made. In your piece of writing you should explain:

- what the critic means by his comment
- whether you think the comment is valid
- why you agree/disagree with the comment
- why Priestley made the decision to present the play in this way.

Stephen Daldry's production

The play has been revived regularly since 1945 but it had a complete 'make-over' in 1992 when theatre director Stephen Daldry more or less re-invented the play for the National Theatre in a production that broke **box-office** records. Since then, thousands of people have seen the 'Daldry' version, as it is a production that has been **touring** off and on for the past 20 years.

box-office where tickets are sold; also used to refer to the amount of money made from ticket sales

coup de théâtre a sudden and unexpected turn of events in a play

critics people who write reviews

debut first performance

touring when a production is performed in different places

If you are lucky enough to see Stephen Daldry's version of the play, you will need to bear in mind that, although Daldry uses Priestley's script, he has made several distinctive changes to the play. In your assessment, don't confuse Priestley's play with Daldry's production.

In Daldry's version the most striking change is the setting, which is expressionistic. The curtains open at the start to show an Edwardian 'dolls house' raised on stilts above the level of the stage, where street urchins are seen playing. At first we only see and hear the family celebration through the windows of the 'dolls house' frontage, before this is pulled away.

Stephen Daldry's set for the 2009 National Theatre Production featured the imposing structure of the Birlings' house raised on stilts on the stage

The Birlings and Gerald are all costumed in typical Edwardian evening dress. However, when the Inspector arrives, he wears a costume that suggests he is from 1945. The audience gradually gathers that the Inspector is a visitor from the future. As the play progresses, there are sound effects of air-raid sirens and films are projected onto the stage, showing footage of war planes. These effects are directly linked to the Inspector's warning of the **'fire and blood and anguish'** *(Act Three)* to come. At the end of the play, the Birlings lose their house and it is seen collapsing and spilling its contents, smashed and broken, onto the stage.

Activity 17

Watch trailers and clips of Stephen Daldry's production on the Internet. Write a short review, either criticizing or supporting Daldry's choices, based on your own interpretation of the play.

Expressionist features of Daldry's production

- **The setting** – an imposing house, raised on stilts, standing in the middle of a wasteland; suggesting a 'dream-like' landscape where the past, present and future converge.
- **Lighting** – the stage was lit using side lighting which illuminates the faces of the characters brightly while maintaining a very dark background – typical of expressionism.
- **Music** – the composer used the theme tune from the Hitchcock thriller film *Vertigo* to create suspense and an atmosphere of foreboding.
- **Performance** – included striking moments of expressionistic action. For example, the Inspector's key speech in Act Three, when he speaks of 'fire and blood and anguish', was delivered directly to the audience rather than to the Birlings to startle them into considering their own responsibilities.
- **Sound** – the use of air-raid sirens and the roar of jet engines was used expressionistically to suggest the danger of the impending war.
- **Costume design** – included two separate dresses for Sheila; one resplendent white, evening gown, bedecked in lace and jewels and a second 'identical' one which had been distressed by the designer to look stained and torn – to express Sheila's internal turmoil and shame as she faces up to her responsibility towards Eva.

Writing about the play in performance

Upgrade

When you are writing about *An Inspector Calls* in the exam, try to remember to write about Priestley's intentions for the 'audience' rather than for the 'reader' as it is the audience that the playwright is addressing. You should also be sensitive to the fact that some aspects of the play are open to multiple interpretations.

Priestley's stage directions offer a valuable insight into his vision regarding how the play should be performed, as well as his overall intentions. You should pay close attention to the stage directions and remember to quote from them if this will help to support your argument.

Even if you do not have an opportunity to see the play at the theatre, you need to think about the effects created for the audience as the action unfolds on stage, and then reflect this in your response.

Remember, however, that you must write about the text as Priestley wrote it and not one particular performance. Do not be tempted to make references to the film versions or to Daldry's 're-invention' of the play, unless you are making a point that is precisely relevant to the question.

Skills for the assessment

There are several practical steps you can take to make sure that you are fully prepared for the challenges of the exam.

Step 1: Make sure you know the play really well

An Inspector Calls is quite a short play so you should try to read it at least three times before your assessment. Try re-reading the episodes that make up each Act as presented in this book (see page 6). After re-reading an episode, pause and note down what strikes you about:

- plot and structure
- context
- characters
- language
- themes
- performance.

Step 2: Revision

Go back through this *Oxford Literature Companion* and check that you have completed all of the activities. Re-read the key quotations from the play which appear in blue text throughout this book and try to learn as many as you can.

Extracts

Practise potential questions; for example, open the play randomly at any page and then write at least one paragraph about the significance of the section in relation to the list of bullet points in Step 1.

Characters

Choose one of the characters from the play to focus on. Practise writing a page or more about how Priestley presents the character and his or her function in the play. Repeat the task for other characters in the play.

Themes

Choose one of the following themes and practise writing a page or more about its importance in the play: truth; secrets/lies; responsibility; duty; blame and guilt; pride and shame; time.

Repeat the task for other themes.

Activity 1

Read the following quotations from the play. For each one, decide which themes the quotation relates to. Give reasons for your choices.

a) **'the famous younger generation who know it all'** *(Mr Birling, Act Three)*

b) **'I don't think we need to discuss it'** *(Mrs Birling, Act Two)*

c) **'don't let's start dodging and pretending now'** *(Sheila, Act Three)*

d) **'Could I have a drink first'** *(Eric, Act Three)*

e) **'she was desperately hard up'** *(Gerald, Act Two)*

Step 3: Improving exam technique

If you are sitting an exam on your set text, brushing up on exam technique is really worth the effort and can make a real difference to your overall grade. Below are some examples of question types that may come up in your exam.

Essay-style questions

Most essay-style questions will ask you to write about plot (the events that take place in the play), structure (how events are organized), characters or themes. Here are some typical essay-style questions, with key words and phrases in bold. This is followed by an explanation of what each question requires.

How does Priestley create a negative audience response to Mrs Birling throughout the play?

This question is about character and the 'how' part of the question is asking you to focus on the playwright's methods. The writer's methods for creating character include:

- what the character looks/sounds like
- what the character says about himself/herself and about others
- what other characters say about the character
- how the character might be compared/contrasted with others
- what the character does – his/her actions and/or reactions in the play
- what kind of language the character uses when speaking.

In this specific question, points should relate to creating a negative audience response to Mrs Birling through these methods.

Activity 2

1. Create a bullet list of factors you would need to consider when writing a response to the following question.

   > Why is Sheila's role important in *An Inspector Calls*?

2. Compare your ideas with other students in your class.

> *An Inspector Calls* is sometimes described as 'a play of contrasts'. **Do you agree** with this description?

This question is about the nature of the play as a whole. 'Do you agree?' means that you should weigh up whether you agree or disagree with the description and provide evidence to support your views. A good way to approach this type of question is to consider the appropriateness of the statement in relation to plot, structure, characters, themes, mood/atmosphere and language.

Activity 3

Create a plan for the example question above, including details and quotations from the text. Try to organize your plan so that related points are grouped together. Possible points to consider include:

- comparison of lives of luxury with the hardship of the working classes
- differences in the attitudes of the Birling family towards Eva's plight
- themes in the play such as shame and blame, rich and poor, responsibility and selfishness
- differences in the behaviour of the older and younger characters
- the tone at the beginning of the play versus the tone at the end.

Extract-based questions

For extract-based questions you should look at past paper questions to familiarize yourself with the type of question that is specific to the exam you are going to take. You will have to practise reading the printed extract carefully and working with the language on a detailed level.

When writing answers to practise extract-based questions, use a pen or highlighter to underline key words and phrases from the extract that strike you as important. It can also be helpful to write very brief notes in the margins to remind you why you decided to pick out the phrases.

Below is an example of how you might begin to highlight an extract.

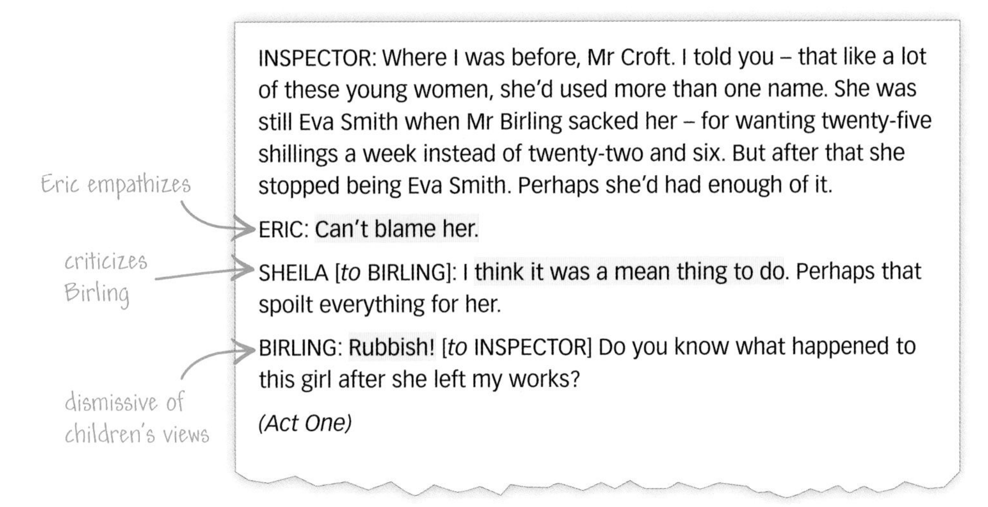

Step 4: Answering the question

Always try to think ahead before you start writing. Thinking and planning ahead will help you to:

- structure your answer logically
- target the precise demands of the question
- avoid missing out points that are crucial to your argument
- include appropriate quotations.

Plans can take a variety of forms. However, a brief list will often be the most helpful as it will allow you to put your ideas into a logical sequence. In an exam, you should plan quickly. Don't spend more than six or seven minutes on a plan. Jot down your ideas and away you go!

Develop your answer, step by step, building your argument by referring to precise moments from the play. Always support your ideas with short, relevant quotations from the play.

The best way to use quotations is to 'embed' them into your own sentences. For example:

> When Gerald challenges the Inspector, telling him 'we're respectable citizens and not criminals' (*Act One*), the Inspector appears unimpressed, replying, 'Sometimes there isn't as much difference as you think', revealing his impressive powers of discernment.

Sample questions

1

Foundation Tier

An Inspector Calls

Either a)

Look at the extract in Act Two beginning with the Inspector's question to Mrs Birling, from the Inspector's line 'You're not even sorry now, when you know what happened to the girl?' to Eric's entrance *'looking extremely pale and distressed'*.

Explore the ways in which Priestley makes this a dramatic and tense section of the play.

You should consider:
- what the characters say and how they say it
- the contrast between the Inspector and the other characters
- Sheila's interruptions.

Or b)
Explore one or two moments in the play when Priestley presents Mr Birling in a particularly negative way.
Remember to support your ideas with details from the play and consider:
- what Mr Birling says and how he says it
- how Mr Birling talks to Eric
- how Mr Birling interacts with the Inspector.

2

Higher Tier

An Inspector Calls

Either a)

Look at the extract in Act Two beginning with the Inspector's question to Mrs Birling, from the Inspector's line 'You're not even sorry now, when you know what happened to the girl?' to Eric's entrance *'looking extremely pale and distressed'*.

Explore the ways in which Priestley makes this a dramatic and tense section of the play.

Or b)
Explore one or two moments in the play when Priestley presents Mr Birling in a particularly negative way.

Remember to support your ideas with details from the play.

3

Foundation Tier

An Inspector Calls

Either a)

How does Priestley present Sheila in *An Inspector Calls*?

You should consider:

- what Sheila says and does
- how other characters respond to her
- the methods Priestley uses to present Sheila.

Or b)

Write about the differences between Gerald Croft and Eric Birling in the play *An Inspector Calls*.

You should write about:

- what they say and do
- their different attitudes
- the methods Priestley uses to present Gerald Croft and Eric Birling.

4

Higher Tier

An Inspector Calls

Either a)

An Inspector Calls exposes a family apparently unaware of their responsibilities to others. How does Priestley present this lack of awareness in the Birling family?

Or b)

How does Priestley use the character of Sheila to reflect his own ideas in the play *An Inspector Calls*?

Sample answers

Sample answer 1

Read the extract below taken from a student response, together with examiner comments, to the following sample **Foundation Tier** question:

> Look at the extract from the end of Act Two, from the Inspector's line 'And you've nothing further to tell me, eh?' to his line 'You're not even sorry now, when you know what happened to the girl?'.
>
> What do you think of the way the Inspector speaks and behaves here?

I think the Inspector is angrier with Mrs Birling than he was with the other characters because she is so stubborn about not being to blame for the death of Eva. Mrs Birling seems to annoy him because she won't face up to what she has done. He loses his temper here a bit.

Abrupt beginning, which lacks context but shows understanding of the Inspector's attitude.

I think Priestley wants us to think that the Inspector is fed up with Mrs Birling for trying to blame Eva herself for her death. The Inspector tells her that it is just as much her responsibility as Eva's as she 'refused it' and he talks about what any normal woman would have done in the situation which would be to be friendly to another woman, especially as she was pregnant and Mrs Birling was a mother herself.

Needs more focus on the Inspector.

The Inspector behaves a bit different with Mrs Birling and tells her 'you slammed the door in her face'. He actually criticizes her harshly here and this makes both Mr Birling and Sheila see that Mrs Birling was horrid to Eva.

A better point: considers the effects of what the Inspector says.

The Inspector also shows a bit of sarcasm when Mrs Birling talks about Eva in a snobbish way calling her 'a girl in her position' suggesting that she had no right to have any 'fine feelings' just because she was working class. The Inspector picks up on Mrs Birling's use of 'position' and is quite snidey when he says 'her position now is that she lies with a burnt-out inside on a slab.' He gets back at Mrs Birling by reminding her and everyone in the room about Eva's horrible death.

Good attention to Priestley's use of tone.

In 1912 it was not polite to refer to 'insides', so this makes the Inspector sound quite rude and angry. He will not cover up the nasty truth but states it clearly.

This point could be developed further.

Good understanding but written style could be better.

Good point, well expressed.

Sensitivity to the language used.

Point could be sharper but shows understanding of the Inspector's perspective.

The Inspector uses shock tactics elsewhere in the play to make the Birlings feel guilty. When Mr Birling tries to stop the Inspector saying more gross things about Eva in the mortuary, the Inspector snaps at him, 'Don't stammer and yammer at me again, man.' I think this really shows how fed up the Inspector is with Mr and Mrs Birling and it is quite rude of the Inspector to call Mr Birling 'man' when he has been a Lord Mayor and magistrate and expects people to treat him with respect not call him 'man' like a common man.

I think it shows how angry the Inspector is getting when he says, 'I'm losing all patience with you' because he sounds like an angry teacher or parent and makes the Birlings seem small. He also asks the question, 'What did she say?' which is printed in italics which shows that on the stage, the Inspector is emphasizing the line with a loud voice or a slow voice to make his point clearer. It upsets Mrs Birling because the stage direction for her is '(rather cowed)' which means even Mrs Birling who is so haughty is a bit shocked by the Inspector.

The Inspector sticks up for Eva throughout this extract. He tries to make Eva sound almost like a mother to the boy who had got her pregnant, calling him 'boy' and 'youngster' instead of a man. This makes Eva sound protective to make Mrs Birling feel guilty when she finds out that it was her son who is to blame for Eva having a baby.

The Inspector is disgusted with Mrs Birling's attitude towards Eva. When he asks Mrs Birling if she is sorry now, it is more of a statement than a question and it shows that the Inspector does not think much of someone who can be so unfeeling when they know about Eva's pain.

This is quite a mixed response. The focus of the answer appears to be directed more towards Mrs Birling than towards the Inspector. Nevertheless, the answer shows some understanding of Priestley's methods and, in the second part, the focus on the Inspector is clearer. This student also uses the text quite well to support the points made.

Sample answer 2

Read the extract below taken from a student response, together with examiner comments, to the following sample **Higher Tier** question:

> What methods does Priestley use in *An Inspector Calls* to highlight the theme of selfishness for the audience?

In 'An Inspector Calls', Priestley uses several methods to highlight the theme of selfishness for the audience.

Clear focus.

One of the most significant methods is Priestley's creation of obviously selfish characters. Mr Birling first reveals his selfishness when he talks about the forthcoming marriage of Sheila and Gerald. Rather than congratulating them or talking about their love for one another, Mr Birling can only see the advantages to himself as he states quite smugly, 'You're just the kind of son-in-law I always wanted' and looks forward to the time when 'Crofts and Birlings... are working together – for lower costs and higher prices.'

Use of judgement shows engagement with the question.

Effective use of quotation from the text.

Another way in which Mr Birling helps to highlight the theme of selfishness is through the repeated use of the personal pronoun 'I', referring to himself, and of 'we', referring either to the Birling family or to fellow capitalists. Even after the Inspector has left the family in Act Three, Mr Birling can only think of himself. When he says, 'I care' the 'caring' is not about the poor dead girl but about his own ruined hopes of a knighthood.

Close focus on language.

Although Sheila is the first person to show her guilt, she is also initially obviously very selfish. For example, her first thought on hearing the news about Eva Smith's painful death is to think of herself, saying 'I wish you hadn't told me' because she finds the news disturbing. We also see how both Gerald and Eric used Eva for their own pleasure without thinking about the potential negative consequences for her.

Relevant point with well-chosen evidence.

The next method that Priestley uses is to show characters discussing selfish and selfless attitudes. For example, just before the arrival of the Inspector, Mr Birling urges the younger men to 'look out' for themselves and their families, and explains that if they do so they won't come to 'much harm'. What Mr Birling fails to tell them, but what the Inspector later reveals, is the harm done to innocent bystanders when people like the Birlings pursue their own selfish aims.

Good focus on Priestley's methods.

Insight into Priestley's use of ideas in the play.

Later in the play, in Act Three, Sheila connects Mr Birling's expression of his selfish view of life with the arrival of the Inspector. She asks in amazement, 'is that when the Inspector came?' This seems to confirm to Sheila and to the audience that the Inspector's real purpose in visiting the Birlings, rather than attempting to solve a mystery, was to educate them about their responsibilities to others and to see the consequences of their selfish attitudes.

Effectively widens the focus to take in the whole play.

The Inspector is also very stern with Mr Birling when he is boasting about his status in Act Two, telling him that 'Public men… have responsibilities as well as privileges'. Here the Inspector is trying to remind Birling that a man of his position – an employer of hundreds of people, a magistrate and former Lord Mayor – should show some concern for people outside his immediate family.

Shows good knowledge of the text.

Unlike Mr Birling, Sheila quickly accepts her responsibility when the Inspector reveals her part in Eva's sad story. She sums up her feelings of guilt about her selfishness in a sarcastic comment that draws attention to Priestley's use of irony. She reacts to the news that the Inspector was an imposter by saying, 'I suppose we're all nice people now', whereas Priestley's whole aim has been to expose this 'nice family' as utterly selfish.

Identifies a further method.

Provides a pithy conclusion.

This is very good work. The candidate works methodically through Priestley's methods and demonstrates detailed knowledge and understanding of the play and its 'mechanics'. This student also shows purposeful use of quotation to support points made.

Glossary

Act the name given to the major divisions of a play

alderman a senior member of a town council

ambiguous where the meaning is not clear or where something has at least two possible meanings

anagnorisis the recognition of the error of one's ways; a feature of Greek tragedy

antagonist the character who opposes the lead character

box-office where tickets are sold; also used to refer to the amount of money made from ticket sales

capitalist society a society where individuals can own and run businesses to make profit; to be successful, business owners must compete to keep costs low while selling their products for the highest possible price

catastrophe in Greek tragedy, the concluding part of a tragedy when the protagonist accepts ruin

catharsis in Greek tragedy, an outrush of emotions as the audience sees the results of the tragedy played out – they pity the broken characters and think about how their actions relate to their own conduct

champion of the poor a supporter of the poor

circular structure a narrative that ends more or less where it begins or which repeats moments of action from the beginning at the end

cliché a 'well-worn' expression or saying that is lacking in originality

cliff-hanger the closing moments of a chapter, scene or episode that ends in suspense, creating anticipation about what will happen next

climax the highest or most intense part of the play or a turning point in the action; a feature of Greek tragedy

colloquial speech informal, everyday speech

complacency a form of self-satisfaction or smugness

contrast ideas and themes that are different from one another or represent opposite perspectives

coup de théâtre a sudden and unexpected turn of events in a play

critics people who write reviews of plays in the theatre

debut first performance

deference an expression of respect shown towards a person deemed to be superior in social rank, wealth or wisdom

denouement resolution of the plot; a feature of Greek tragedy

dramatic irony where the audience have greater knowledge than the characters on stage, enabling them to judge and react to events based on superior understanding

etiquette the rules about what is considered to be 'good manners' within polite sections of society

euphemism a word or phrase used in place of one that might be considered offensive or indelicate in good company

everywoman like 'everyman', a representative of all human beings

exposition key information to help the audience make sense of the play; a feature of Greek tragedy

expressionism an expressionistic setting is likely to be abstract; for example, the set may represent certain themes of the play or attempt to portray the inner feelings of individual characters

figurative language the term for any kind of phrase or sentence that is not literal; figurative language includes metaphors and similes

foil a character whose function is to serve as a contrast to another character

foreground to focus on and bring to the attention of the audience

hierarchy a system of putting people into ranks, with some having superiority and authority over others

hubris excessive pride that ultimately leads to a character's downfall; a feature of Greek tragedy

hypocrisy a form of insincerity; somebody who is hypocritical is a person whose actions are very different from his or her stated beliefs

irony a literary technique where the intended meaning differs from what is said or presented directly

juxtaposition placing two images or ideas side-by-side to highlight the differences between them

linear structure a straightforward, chronological narrative that has a beginning, middle and an end – in that order

Lord Mayor somebody elected to be head of local government in a large city

magistrate a person who acts as a judge in a magistrates' court, dealing with minor offences

manifesto for change a published statement outlining political plans for change

National Health Service a national service introduced in 1948 to provide free medical care for all British citizens

nemesis in Greek tragedy, a person or force that inflicts punishment or revenge

off-stage action that is referred to or reported by characters on-stage, but is not physically shown on stage; such as Eva's death

on the Bench refers to being a magistrate in a magistrates' court, or as it was called in 1912, the police court

parlour maids women employed by wealthy families to wait on the family and their guests in the parlour (reception room); their responsibilities included setting and clearing the table, serving food and opening the door to guests

peripeteia a reversal of fortunes just as a positive outcome had seemed possible; a feature of Greek tragedy

perspective a point of view

proleptic irony occurs when a character says something that turns out to be wrong or more significant than he or she thought at the time

props the moveable objects used on stage by the actors

protagonist the main character

Received Pronunciation the term used for a standard English accent, with no trace of a regional influence; it is sometimes called 'the Queen's English'

selective realism a setting where only the props and furniture that are needed, used or referred to in the play appear on stage and there is no attempt to create the impression of completely realistic surroundings

sarcasm a tone of voice often used in a mocking way, suggesting that the speaker is not sincere in what he or she is saying

script a play becomes a script when it is being used by the production team in rehearsal for a performance

slang distinctive phrases and vocabulary shared by a particular group of people

social reform changes to improve the conditions in which people live and work

socialist society a society that is based on the cooperative ownership and running of businesses, where profits are shared among all the people involved

strike to stop working for a fixed or unlimited time in order to protest against low pay or unfair treatment

subvert to undermine or challenge expectations

sympathetic character a character that the audience can identify with and that therefore makes a positive impression

theatrical realism where the setting attempts to represent real life on stage, with detailed sets and convincing surroundings

United Nations a multi-national committee founded in 1945, following the Second World War, with the aim of preventing further wars between countries

triple a 'triple' is a literary device that uses the combination of three short related statements, adjectives or adverbs to add emphasis to an idea or argument

touring when a production is performed in different places

unsympathetic character a character who makes a negative impression on the audience

vagrant a tramp, with no home and no work

Great Clarendon Street, Oxford OX2 6DP

Oxford University Press is a department of the University of Oxford. It furthers the University's objective of excellence in research, scholarship, and education by publishing worldwide in

Oxford New York

Auckland Cape Town Dar es Salaam Hong Kong Karachi
Kuala Lumpur Madrid Melbourne Mexico City Nairobi
New Delhi Shanghai Taipei Toronto

With offices in

Argentina Austria Brazil Chile Czech Republic France Greece
Guatemala Hungary Italy Japan Poland Portugal Singapore
South Korea Switzerland Thailand Turkey Ukraine Vietnam

Oxford is a registered trade mark of Oxford University Press in the UK and in certain other countries

© Su Fielder 2013

The moral rights of the author have been asserted

Database right Oxford University Press (maker)

First published 2013

All rights reserved. No part of this publication may be reproduced, stored in a retrieval system, or transmitted, in any form or by any means, without the prior permission in writing of Oxford University Press, or as expressly permitted by law, or under terms agreed with the appropriate reprographics rights organization. Enquiries concerning reproduction outside the scope of the above should be sent to the Rights Department, Oxford University Press, at the address above

You must not circulate this book in any other binding or cover and you must impose this same condition on any acquirer

British Library Cataloguing in Publication Data

Data available

ISBN 978-0-19-839041-1

10 9 8 7 6 5 4 3

Printed in China by Printplus

Acknowledgements
The publisher and author are grateful for permission to reprint the following copyright material:

Extracts from *An Inspector Calls* by J B Priestley (Penguin, 2000), reprinted by permission of United Agents on behalf of The Estate of the late J B Priestley

Cover: THEPALMER/iStock; **p7:** Robert Day; **p8:** Monkey Business Images/Shutterstock; **p11:** AF archive/Alamy; **p15:** Donald Cooper/Photostage; **p17:** Richard Thornton/Shutterstock; **p19:** karambol/iStock; **p22:** Bettina Strenske/Alamy; **p24:** Mary Evans/Everett Collection; **p25:** The Bridgeman Art Library Ltd./Alamy; **p31:** Amoret Tanner/Alamy; **p32:** iww.org; **p34:** INTERFOTO/Alamy; **p38:** Robert Day; **p43:** Donald Cooper/Photostage; **p44:** Donald Cooper/Photostage; **p47:** Donald Cooper/Photostage; **p51:** Tristram Kenton/The Guardian; **p52:** thislife pictures/Alamy; **p56:** Donald Cooper/Photostage; **p59:** AF archive/Alamy; **p62:** Kuzma/Shutterstock; **p65:** Amoret Tanner/Alamy; **p69:** Donald Cooper/Photostage; **p72:** Robert Day; **p75:** Mary Evans Picture Library; **p77:** Pressmaster/Shutterstock; **p79:** AF archive/Alamy; **p82:** Donald Cooper/Photostage